Hot Issues Today

Edited & Annotated
by
Choi, In-Soon

최인순

이화여자대학교 문리대 영문과 졸업
Loyola University of Chicago 영문학 석사
University of Wisconsin 영문학 박사
현재 서경대학교 인문대학 영어과 교수

Hot Issues Today

First Published Feb. 2010
Second Published Feb. 2013
SHINASA Publishing Co.
28-36 NokBeon-Dong, EunPyung-Gu, Seoul, Korea
Registered : 9-52 (Jan. 5 1956)
Tel : 02-382-6411
Fax : 02-382-6401
E-mail : shinasa@chol.com / Homepage : www.shinasa.co.kr

ISBN : 978-89-8396-684-1

Printed and bounded in Korea

₩10,000

Contents

Contents

Section Six: Feminism

Section Seven: Great Speeches

Section One

BUSINESS

1. Cubicle, sweet Cubicle

Michele Weldon

1. Very few[1] employees get the corner office with the panoramic skyline view anymore. What's more likely to[2] happen is we sink into[3] tiny, homogeneous* cubicles every morning. Some even toil in offices embracing "hoteling," in which workers have only temporary* claim to a desk or work area on a first-come, first-served basis.[4]

2. "In a cubicle* environment*, it is much more difficult. Status gets mowed down.[5] The uniformity takes away a person's uniqueness. There is this openness with no privacy, which is a limitation of sanctuary*," says Dan Conti, a psychologist and director of the employee assistance program at First Chicago NBD Corp.

3. How can you do your job well in these privacy-impaired* work spaces and still feel comfortable and productive?

homogeneous [hòumədʒíːniəs]: the same, (opp.) heterogeneous
temporary [témpərèri]: 일시적인, 임시의: (opp.) permanent
cubicle [kjúːbikl]: 칸막이한 작은 방, (도서관의) 개인 열람실.
environment [inváiərənmənt]: 환경
sanctuary [sǽŋktʃuəri]: 신전(神殿), 성역
impair [impέər]: 손상시키다, 악화시키다

---

1) very few: (부정) 거의 없다
2) be likely to~: 있음직하다, ~ 할 것 같다
be more likely to~: 더 있음직하다
3) sink into: stay and become very involved: 푹 주저앉다
4) first-come, first-served basis: arranged or done in the order that people arrive
5) mowed down: cut down

4. Working at tuning out[1] the surrounding noises and intensely focusing on the task at hand[2] works for some.[3] "The best source of distraction* is pouring yourself into[4] your work," says Conti.

5. "I would not focus on the cubicle, I would focus on the work," agrees Marsha Sinetar, author of "To Build The Life You Want, Create The Work You Love: The Spiritual Domain* of Entrepreneuring*" (St. Martin's/Griffin, $9.95) and president and founder of Sinetar Associates, in Santa Rosa, Calif., specializing in strategic[5] planning, marketing and leadership consulting.

6. In a beehive[6] existence, the lack of a privacy zone where you can concentrate and de-stress without public scrutiny* presents a substantial* challenge. The relentless* exposure* to others' chatter* and personal and professional business also is draining*. Conti recommends brief breaks, whether to lunch with non-work friends, walk around the office or stroll* outside, to supply some mental respite*.

distraction [distrǽkʃən]: ① 주의 산만, 방심 ② 기분 전환, 머리를 식히는 일. 여기서는 ② 의 뜻
domain [douméin]: 영역, 분야, (책임의) 범위
entrepreneur [ɑ̀:ntrəprənə́:]: 사업가, 기업가
scrutiny [skrú:təni]: 정밀조사, 철저한 검토
substantial [səbstǽnʃəl]: 상당한
relentless [riléntlis]: 가차 없는, 혹독한
exposure [ikspóuʒər]: 노출
chatter [tʃǽtər]: 수다(를 떨다), 재잘거리다
drain [drein]: 물을 빼내다, 물이 빠지다, 배수관
stroll [stroul]: 산책(하다), 거닐다
respite [réspit]: 일시적인 중단, 한숨 돌리기

1) tuning out: ignoring
2) the task at hand: work that must be done immediately
3) working and focusing (s.) — works (v.)
4) pour yourself into ~: ~ 에 완전 몰두하다
5) strategic: strategy의 adj., 전략적
6) beehive: a structure in which bees are kept

7. A code of cubicle conduct[1] also can help you and your open-neighbors coexist harmoniously. Keep your voice moderated[2] and accord[3] others at least the illusion of privacy by not[4] jumping into[5] conversations or responding to what you've heard them speak about on the phone. Also, respect boundaries* by sending others electronic messages when appropriate[6] instead of constantly intruding* on their area.

8. To remind yourself of your roles outside the work environment, include photographs of your family or your favorite rose garden on your desk. Also, a "simple splash* of humor" via cartoons or sayings* in your cubicle can help keep your work life in perspective.[7]

9. Design experts say there are also simple ways to make your work space more appealing. "The more pleasing, the more organized and the more aesthetic* (your space) is, the more together[8] you're going to be,[9]" says Celeste Cooper, creative director of Repertoire, a design firm with offices in Boston and New York. For example, improving your "deskscape"[10] with black-and-white desk accessories and a framed black-and-white photograph can help your attitude as well as neutralize* the impact of an odious* cubicle color, Cooper says.

boundary [báundəri]: 경계(선), 분계선
intrude [intrú:d]: 자기 마음대로 가다, 침범하다
splash [splæʃ]: 철벅 하는 소리, 철벅 떨어지다
saying [séiiŋ]: 속담, 격언
aesthetic [esθétik]: 심미적, 미학적 (특질)
neutralize [njú:trəlàiz]: 무효화시키다, 상쇄시키다

1) code of conduct: an informal set of rules for behavior cf.) dress code
2) moderated: not loud
3) accord: ① agree, concur ② bestow, confer 여기서는 ② 의 뜻
4) by not ~: ~ 하지 않음으로써
5) jumping into: quickly and thoughtlessly joining an activity
6) when (it is) appropriate
7) keep in perspective: know what is really important in life
8) together: emotionally healthy and well-organized
9) the more ~, the more —: ~ 하면 할수록, 더욱 — 하다
10) deskscape: desk + landscape 합성어

10. A low level of clutter* also counts.[1] "People tend to have clear thoughts when it is all in order," says Rita Falkner, president of FSI of New York Ltd., a design firm.

11. Eclectic* and interesting desk accessories such as handmade pottery can infuse* style, says Trina Catania, owner of Catania Executive Gifts, a gift company in Chicago.

12. Yet overdoing the decorating in your cubicle can be as big a problem as having an anonymous*, lifeless spot. It is inappropriate to exceed your space with plants or large frames that rise above the top or exceed the width of your cubicle. Resist the urge to fill every square inch[2] with a personal memento*. "Every office needs 'rest walls' or blank space to look at," says Linda Marder, principal in her own design firm in Los Angeles.

13. After a full day of working in your cubicle or desk in an open area, Conti says, it is imperative* to recuperate* from a sense of always "being in the middle of it,[3]" with time spent alone in your home.

14. The proper attitude is also important, Sinetar advises. "If working in a cubicle is your biggest problem, then you are blessed."

odious [óudiəs]: 끔찍한, 혐오스러운
clutter [klʌ́tər]: 채우다, 집어넣다, 잡동사니, 어수선함
eclectic [ekléktik]: 취사선택하는, 절충하는
infuse [infjú:z]: 주입하다, 불어넣다
anonymous [ənάnəməs]: 익명의
memento [miméntou]: 기념품
imperative [impérətiv]: 반드시 해야 하는, 긴요한 (것)
recuperate [rikjú:pərèit]: 회복하다, 되찾다

1) count: matter, be important
2) square inch: a square with sides of one inch
3) be in the middle of it: be very involved in busy activity

2. Companies that still make people—not profit—top priority

Carol Kleman

1. Workers at the Wilton Conner Packaging Co. in Charlotte, N.C.,[1] get their laundry* done[2] on the premises[3] for $1 a load.

2. Federal Express Corp.[4] in Memphis names planes for employees' children.

3. Silicon Graphics Inc.[5] of Mountain View, Calif., allows water fights at the end of major projects.

4. John Nuveen Co. in Chicago pays college tuition* for children of long-term employees.

5. And, at Open Market, a Boston consulting firm,[6] employees can bring their dogs to work.

6. What's going on here?[7] Don't these companies know that the rest of the corporate world has, seemingly,[8] declared* war on employees?

7. Why are they being so nice?

laundry [lɔ́:ndri]: 세탁물
tuition [tju:íʃən]: 수업료, 교습비
declare [diklέər]: 선언하다, 공표하다

1) N. C.: North Carolina 주
2) get something done: do or finish something
3) on the premises: at the place itself
4) Corp.: Corporation 의 약자
5) Inc.: Incorporated 의 약자: 주식회사 (주로 영식), Ltd. (미식)
6) firm; company
7) What's going on?: What's happening?
8) seemingly: 겉으로는, 표면적으로는

8. Despite extensive downsizing at many companies — and the feeling of alienation* among remaining employees — the "most progressive companies today don't stop at focusing on profit; they're also focusing on the profit-makers: the employees."

9. So says Jim Harris of Indian Rocks Beach, Fla.,[1] a management consultant* who specializes in "high performance management" and is president of the firm that bears his name.[2]

10. Harris, whose client base includes Fortune 500 companies,[3] also is the author of "Getting Employees to Fall in Love With Your Company" (AMACOM, $17.95), a book that surprises in today's anorexic* job market because it encourages employers to be kind to employees if they want to retain[4] them.

11. "America's No. 1 business problem is not generating profit,[5] because we have become brilliant at squeezing pennies[6] to the bottom line," said Harris, who has a doctorate[7] in speech communications from the University of Florida. "The problem today is how to maintain a loyal, committed work force. Companies that have the attitude that employees don't matter[8] are losing their best workers."

12. The solution is for employers to capture workers' hearts, Harris says. "Excellence isn't possible with a disengaged heart.[9] If employers don't do that, they are merely creating an environment of warm bodies."

alienation [èiljənéiʃən]: 소외
consultant [kənsʌltənt]: 상담가, 자문 위원
anorexic [æ̀nəréksik]: 신경성 식욕 부진증, 거식증 환자

1) Fla.: Florida 주
2) bear a name: have the same name as someone
3) Fortune 500 companies: the top 500 U.S. corporations compiled and published by *Fortune* magazine
4) retain [ritéin]: 유지하다, 보유하다
5) generating (동명사) = to generate
6) squeeze pennies: be very careful about expenses
7) doctorate: Ph. D. degree (Doctor of Philosophy): 박사학위
8) matter: be important
9) with disengaged heart: 마음이 떠나서

13. Harris knows labor market realities. "My career is typical*," he said. "In the 1980s, I was outplaced, downsized and fired from three major U. S. corporations. All three were the result of corporate reorganization.[1] I understand the tenuous* relationship that exists between employees and management."

14. Harris counsels his corporate clients not to forget that "the only competitive advantage in the next decade isn't marketing or technology—anybody can buy those. The real edge[2] is the quality of your work force: Can you retain the best and the brightest?"

15. Though cynical* observers might point out[3] to Harris that urging companies to use positive reinforcement*[4] to motivate their employees might be like installing wall-to-wall[5] carpeting on the Titanic, Harris says employees will respond.

16. He also says he has a data base of hundreds of examples of companies trying to establish a happy workplace, among them the "most successful and profitable companies," such as Southwest Airlines, which calls its human resource department the "People Department"; Home Depot Inc.; Ben & Jerry's Homemade Inc.; and North American Tool & Dye Co.

17. "Loyalty isn't dead," said Harris, referring to employers and workers. "It's just being re-defined."

18. The Society for Human Resource Management, based in Alexandria, Va.,[6] also sees the value of[7] happy employees. "Innovative employee benefits incorporate changing lifestyles and allow companies to attract and retain talented employees,[8]" it concludes in its survey of 308 association members.

typical [típikəl]: 전형적인. 대표적인 / tenuous [ténjuəs]: 미약한, 보잘것없는
cynical [sínikəl]: 냉소적인 / reinforcement [rì:infɔ́:rsmənt]: 증강 병력, 증원 요원

1) corporate reorganization: 구조 조정
2) edge: 여기서는, advantage 의 뜻
3) point out to ~: ~ 에게 지적, 언급하다
4) positive reinforcement: 칭찬, 격려의 뜻
5) wall-to-wall: 바닥을 다 덮는
6) Va.: Virginia 주
7) see the value of ~: appreciate ~
8) benefits (s.) --- incorporate and allow (v.) 의 문장구조

19. Family-friendly[1] benefits are the way to achieve employee satisfaction, the Society says. Fifty percent of the firms offer flex[2] time; 24 percent, job sharing; 23 percent, compressed* work weeks; and 20 percent, child care referral and telecommuting.
20. But telecommuting may be a problem: If you work from home, can you bring your dog to the office?

compress [kəmprés]: 압축하다, 꾹 누르다

1) family-friendly: 가족친화적인
2) flex: flexible

Section Two

Lifestyle & Art

1. The Delights of Downsizing

Advice for the simple life: Try parenthood

Robert Hughes

1. When I first read about the lifestyle trend* of the '90s called Voluntary Simplicity, I let out[1] an involuntary chuckle that traveled right through a cackle into an involuntary guffaw.[2]

2. "Ha!" I laughed as I read the stories about the couples who have given up their stressful high-paying jobs and "downshifted" to living the simple life on the interest from their investments*, clipping coupons from the supermarket, baking their own bread and keeping up a high profile of conspicuous* smugness.[3]

3. How sad, how retro[4], how hopelessly out of step,[5] for without fanfare* and press releases*, my wife and I find ourselves several laps* ahead of this movement, having long ago passed up Voluntary Simplicity and systematically downshifted to a better and simpler way of life.

trend [trend]: 동향, 추세
investment [invéstmənt]: 투자
conspicuous [kənspíkjuəs]: 눈에 잘 띄는, 튀는, 뚜렷한

fanfare [fǽnfεər]: 팡파르, 대대적인 축하
release [rilíːs]: 풀어 주다, 석방(하다)
lap [læp]: [경기] 랩, (주로(走路)의) 한 바퀴, 한 왕콕

1) let out: express, (소리를) 지르다, 입밖에 내다
2) chuckle: a quiet laugh < cackle: a high, sharp laugh < guffaw: a loud burst of laughter
3) keep up — conspicuous smugness: buy expensive things in order to appear wealthy
4) retro: old-fashioned
5) out of step: not fashionable

4. Stage 1: The Marriage Downshift.

5. Before we were married, Ellen and I had every reason to believe that we had a life of luxury and ease ahead. Visiting our multiple residences throughout the year, keeping a watchful eye on[1] our polo ponies and driving our behemoth[2] off-the-road vehicles to ski resorts were just some of the activities we used to fantasize about while sipping strong coffee in her tiny studio apartment.

6. But realizing in advance the sheer* stress and shallowness of this sort of crass* consumption*, we opted for a more spiritual existence by downshifting to the plane of ordinary married folk.

7. Stage 2: The Parenting Downshift.

8. When we were first married, we looked around us at our lifestyle with its nights out at the latest films, its uninterrupted conversations, its several working household appliances, and knew there had to be less.

9. Living for ourselves and our possessions was cloying* and dishonest. The simple needs and simple smiles of children were what we needed to gain perspective and prioritize our values.[3]

10. When we look back on it, the fascinating lifestyle aspect of the decision to have children is this: It is the last voluntary thing we have ever done.

11. Stage 3: The Involuntary Downshift.

12. Before parenthood, our two-bedroom house seemed unnecessarily opulent* and vast, like Citizen Kane's Xanadu.[4] The arrival of our

sheer [ʃiə:r]: 순전한, 수직으로
crass [kræs]: 무신경한
consumption [kənsʌ́mpʃən]: 소비, 소모
cloy [klɔi]: 물리다, 질리다
opulent [ɑ́pjələnt]: 호화로운

1) keep a watchful eye on: take good care of
2) behemoth: (성서에 나오는 하마(hippopotamus)와 같은) 거수
3) prioritize our values: arrange according to importance
4) Citizen Kane: a 1941 American film, directed by and starring Orson Welles
Xanadu: 영화에 등장하는 대저택

two little boys, now aged 5 and 7, solved this problem brilliantly, freeing us from bourgeois reliance* on open space, unbroken furniture and Lego-free[1)] carpeting.

13. Today when I walk into the home of someone with young children and my host feels no need to warn me about the chair I'm about to[2)] sit on, I know I'm in the house of someone who badly needs a good downshifting.

14. The beauty of this stage is that you feel like you've moved to a smaller house without actually buying one. Each room seems about half its original size, and all this happened without having to deal with real estate agents.

15. Stage 4: The Undersizing Downshift.

16. The big problem with the Voluntary Simplicity movement is that it doesn't go far enough—the rich downshift[3)] to just the right point to fulfill basic needs. True simplicity, however, means going past that point.

17. For instance, they never seem to drive truly downsized cars. I do. Our sometimes reliable[4)] 1988 Escort, like-new in that[5)] about 30 percent of its working parts have been replaced, takes a certain amount of social courage to drive.

18. When my sons say things like, "Why do we drive such a stupid car, Dad?" I smile and reply that they will understand when they grow up. For the truth is, when I look up at the gleaming* mini-vans that pass us on the highway, I'm proud to know I'm in the company of Gandhi, St. Francis, Buddha and other non-materialist giants of history.

19. Stage 5: Absolute Simplicity.

reliance [riláiəns]: 의존, 의지
gleam [gli:m]: 어슴푸레 빛나다, 어슴푸레한 빛

1) ~-free: ~ 로부터 자유로운, ~ 없는
cf.) smoke-free zone: 금연구역
2) be about to ~: be going to ~, 막 ~ 하려고하다
3) the rich (people) (s.) — downshift (v.) 의 문장구조
4) sometimes reliable: most of the times unreliable
5) like-new in that —: —라는 면에서 새 것 같은

20. Formerly wealthy downshifters always note that they now have more time for things that really matter to them, like long walks at sunset, discussing books with friends and preparing **elaborate*** meals from vegetables grown in their own gardens.

21. Read a book? Grow a vegetable? Take a walk? The child-down-shifted household **eliminates*** all these confusing choices that cause stress in modern life.

22. These days, for example, my wife and I can relax in the knowledge that every evening for the **foreseeable*** future will be spent doing homework. We will sit patiently through hour after hour of quality time, enriching our children with our extensive knowledge of 2nd, 3rd, and 4th grade math, modeling for them the advice of Henry David Thoreau[1] to "simplify, simplify, simplify."

23. The downwardly mobile[2] **aristocracy*** has a lot to learn from us, the absolutely simple folks.[3] They should watch us carefully for the next lifestyle trend. From what I hear about raising teenagers, we just might push through the outside of the envelope[4] and into Total Complexity.

24. Stay tuned.[5]

elaborate [ilǽbərit]: 정교한, 공들인; [~èit]: 공들이다
eliminate [ilímənèit]: 없애다, 제거하다
foreseeable [fɔːrsíːəbl]: 예측할 수 있는
aristocracy [æ̀rəstɑ́krəsi]: 귀족 (계층)

1) Henry David Thoreau: 미국의 철학자 · 시인 · 수필가 (1817-1862)
2) downwardly mobile: (opp.) upwardly mobile
3) us와 folks는 동격
4) push the envelope: go to the limit or stretch the limit
5) stay tuned: 채널을 고정하다

2. Art, Photography, Copyright and the Law

Constance L. Hays

1. Three years ago, the artist Jeff Koons, who had decided to create a sculpture called "String of Puppies," sent a greeting card that he had bought in an airport gift shop to his workers in Italy, telling them that the sculpture "must be just like photo" on the card.

2. The photograph, which featured a couple holding eight German shepherd puppies, became the model for four Koons sculptures, three of which sold for a total of S367,000 after being shown at the Sonnabend Gallery in Manhattan.

3. Koons's supporters applauded*. Art Rogers sued.

4. It was Rogers's photograph that Koons used—without permission—in what Rogers called an infringement* on his copyright.

5. Now, the art world and copyright lawyers are watching an appeal of Rogers's original lawsuit, which they say raises some critical questions: What is art? At what point does artistic freedom end and copyright infringement begin? And will enforcing* copyright restrictions deprive artists of their First Amendment rights?[1]

applaud [əplɔ́:d]: 박수를 치다
infringement [infríndʒmənt]: 위반, 침해
enforce [enfɔ́:rs]: 집행하다, 강요[강제]하다, 강행하다

1) deprive A of B: A 에게서 B 를 빼앗다

6. In some ways, they say, the court is being asked to help determine the legitimacy* of a fairly recent genre in which items from popular culture are borrowed and sometimes reshaped to make social criticisms.

7. "This is a difficult case because there are First Amendment[1)] issues on both sides," said Kathleen M. Sullivan, a Harvard law School professor who has testified* in similar art cases. "Will the Rogerses of the world be intimidated* if they're not protected from theft, or will the Koonses of the world be stymied* because their sources are cut off? It's a toss-up.[2)]"

8. Last December. a federal judge in Manhattan agreed with Rogers, who is a photographer in California. The judge ruled[3)] that Koons, who faces similar charges in three other lawsuits, had used Rogers's work in a way that violated copyright laws.

9. But because Rogers and Koons sought a ruling but not a trial,[4)] the judge said he could not decide if Rogers should receive damages, namely[5)] part of the $367,000 paid for the three sold statues.

10. Neither side was happy and both appealed the lower court[6)] ruling. The appeal is to be heard[7)] next month in the U.S. Court of Appeals[8)] for the 2d Circuit in Manhattan.

legitimacy [lidʒítəməsi]: 타당성, 합법성, 정당성
testify [téstəfài]: 증언하다, 진술하다
intimidate [intímədèit]: 겁을 주다, 위협하다
stymie, stymy [stáimi]: 방해하다, 좌절시키다

1) First Amendment to the U. S. Constitution protects religious freedom, guarantees free speech, freedom of the press and assembly and the right to petition the government.
2) toss-up: 동전던지기로 정하기: 50-50 chance
3) rule: 판결하다
4) ruling: (특히 판사의) 결정, 판결
trial: 공판, 재판, 심리
5) namely: that is to say: 즉, 다시 말하자면
6) lower court: 하급 법정
7) hear: [법률]진술을 듣다; (사건 따위를) 심리하다, 신문하다.
8) Court of Appeals: 미국의) 상소 법원, (주(州)의) 제2심 법원

11. "The lower court simply did not understand the social critique that is embedded* in this artistic tradition," said Michael D. Rips, one of the lawyers representing Koons.

12. "Basically, these artists see society as overrun[1] by consumerism. They pull items out of mass culture and comment critically on those items. It's not something judges are terribly familiar with, and part of the process in Koons's case is educating the judges."

13. To Koons, his lawyers said, the photograph of the couple and puppies was part of the wide trough* of American popular culture from which he draws inspiration. Rogers's photography simply happened to be[2] the image that he chose for his sculpture, his lawyers said, after more than two years of collecting similar images in notebooks.

14. Rogers disagrees, of course. He said he felt "totally ripped off[3]" after seeing a photograph of Koons's work, which had many similarities to his own.

15. "This is elevating[4] stealing to some level of art," said Rogers, who produces a weekly photo column called the Point Reyes Family Album for a newspaper in Point Reyes, California.

16. "Nothing is sacred to Koons. No one has any privacy, any rights, because he is parodying it as a great artist who can do this in the name of[5] art. Can he kill somebody in the name of art? Where do you draw the line?[6]"

17. In his lawsuit, Rogers accused Koons of "reappropriation*,[7]"

embed [imbéd]: 박다, 끼워 넣다
trough [trɔ(:)f]: 구유, 여물통
reappropriation [riəpróuprièiʃən]: 재도용, 재전용

---

1) overrun: 급속히 퍼지다, 가득 차다
2) happen to be ~: 마침, 공교롭게도 ~ 이다
3) ripped off: cheated, robbed
rip ~ off: ~에게 바가지를 씌우다/ rip-off: 바가지
4) elevating = to elevate (SVC 의 문장구조)
5) in the name of: for the sake of
6) draw the line: set the limit
7) accuse A of B: A 를 B 의 일로 고소, 비난하다

saying that although the photograph of the puppies was public, it had been copyrighted and was protected against **unauthorized*** use.

18. Just how much Koons transformed the photograph is part of the debate. Koons's lawyers contend that by creating a sculpture, Koons developed a whole new form.

19. They added that the addition of colors and other details—like daisies **sprouting*** from the people's hair and ears, and a bright blue cast on the puppies—distinguished his sculptures even further from the photograph.[1] At the same time, they say, using Italian artisans who normally carve crucifixes and church sculptures elevated the image to **beatific*** heights, "like a Pieta."

20. Moreover, jeff Koons and his lawyers say, even if Rogers wanted to create his own sculpture based on "Puppies," there would be no loss to him because it would be an Art Rogers, not a Jeff Koons.

21. Others are less convinced. "Basically, he has **appropriated*** somebody else's work for his own use," said Stephen E. Weil, an author of books on art law and a deputy director of the Hirschhom Museum and Sculpture Garden in Washington.

22. "It would be **preposterous*** to think that you could write a novel, and then somebody else could come along and break it up into a lot of short stories and say it's a totally different thing."

23. Much of the **controversy*** seems to stem from[2] disagreement about Koons's art. His supporters depict him as a **wunderkind***

unauthorized [ʌnɔ́:θəràizd]: 공인되지 않은, 승인되지 않은
sprout [spraut]: 싹이 나다, 발아하다, 자라기 시작하다
beatific [bì:ətífik]: 기쁨이 넘치는, 더없이 행복해 하는
appropriate [əpróuprièit]: 적절한, 도용하다, 전용하다
preposterous [pripɑ́stərəs]: 말도 안 되는, 터무니없는
controversy [kɑ́ntrəvə̀:rsi]: 논란, 논쟁
wunderkind [vúndə:rkìnd]: wonder child: 신동, 귀재

1) distinguish A from B: A 를 B 와 구별 지우다
2) stem from ~: ~에서 유래하다, 일어나다

whose stark* postmodernism descends from the best in American and European art. His critics call him market-driven,[1] among other things.[2]

24. Koons, a former Wall Street trader, made a name for himself[3] in the 1980s by encasing vacuum cleaners in Plexiglas boxes and casting stainless-steel replicas of inflatable rabbits.

25. Such a tradition can be linked to artists like Marcel Duchamp, his lawyers argue, who set the Paris art world on its ear[4] at the turn of the century[5] by placing a urinal in a major exhibition.

26. There are also ties to Andy Warhol, they say, who transformed a modest can of soup into something to grace the living room walls.

27. "Since 1979, Koons has been making art that provokes thought," wrote Michael Danoff in a catalog for a Koons show at the Museum of Contemporary Art in Chicago. "Koons communicates through a heightened sense of symbolism. He attaches a profusion* of meaning to the things he sees and likewise to those objects he presents as art."

28. Yve-Alain Bois, a professor of modern art at Harvard University, disagrees. "As far as my own judgment,[6]" he said, "his work is totally trivial* and a pure product of the market. He's considered to be an heir to Duchamp, but I think it's a trivialization of all that. I think he's kind of[7] a commercial artist."

stark [stɑːrk]: 순전한, 홀랑 벗은, 삭막 [황량]한
profusion [prəfjúːʒən]: 다량, 풍성함
trivial [tríviəl]: 하찮은, 대단치 않은

1) market-driven: primarily concerned with selling things
2) among other things (others): 많은 가운데, 그 중에서도 특히
3) made a name for himself: became famous
4) set ~ on its ear: make ~ excited: 흥분시키다
5) at the turn of the century: 새로운 세기가 시작될 때
6) is concerned 혹은 goes 생략됨
7) kind of: sort of: 일종의 ('하찮은' 의 의미 내포)

29. Amid so many flaring* opinions, the case of Art Rogers vs.[1] Jeff Koons and Sonnabend Gallery will try[2] for a resolution* in the appeals court. Meanwhile, the fourth version of “String of Puppies” languishes* in a warehouse, under court order.

flaring [flέəriŋ]: 활활 타는, 현란한
resolution [rèzəlúːʃ-ən]: 결의, 결의안 [문]
languish [lǽŋgwiʃ]: (쇠)약해지다, 시들다

1) vs.: versus: 【L.】 against
2) try: [법률] 재판에 부치다, (사건을) 심리, 심문하다

3. National Cliché or Good Metaphor?

Don Oldenburg

1. Soon after his wedding 25 years ago, Martin Gannon knew something was not quite right. Every night he would watch patiently as his bride ate in virtual* silence. He did not know why — not until 14 years later, when the young business professor moved his family to Kassel, Germany, to do research under a Fulbright fellowship.

2. His wife, Doris, then and still[1] thoroughly* American, looked forward to spending a year in the country where she was born and raised before moving to the United States at age 9.

3. "I found that my wife was more similar to the Germans than she was[2] to the Americans," said Mr. Gannon, who quickly recognized his own dinner behavior to be at odds with[3] a nation of people who see eating as a most serious business. "I happen to be Irish-American,[4] and the Irish really don't eat that way. Food is secondary to conversation for them."

virtual [və́:rtʃuəl]: 사실상의, 거의 ~과 다름없는
thoroughly [θə́:rəli]: 완전히, 철저히

---

1) then and still: 그때도 그리고 여전히
2) she was (similar 생략)
3) be at odds with ~: ~와 충돌하다, ~와 사이가 좋지 않다
4) happen to be ~: 마침, 공교롭게도 ~ 이다

4. If quiet meals proved to be[1] a minor cultural clash in an otherwise[2] harmonious marriage, they also started Martin Gannon thinking about cultural mind-sets,[3] about how people in a society think, feel and act purely because they are members of that society.

5. Three years ago, after an extended stay in Bangkok, he felt he had found a way to characterize behavior in terms to promote understanding: metaphors. He fashioned a seminar to pursue such culturally potent* metaphors at the University of Maryland.

6. Aided by graduate students, many of them foreigners, he explored ways in which to characterize diverse societies. The three-year effort has produced a 500-page manuscript whose table of contents[4] is a collection of image-inducing entries such as the Mexican Fiesta and Belgian Lace.

7. Using metaphors as a serious way to describe societies is relatively new, Mr. Gannon said. He credits anthropologists* with experimenting with the device, and organizational theorists with applying it in their field[5] (the organization as "machine," for instance). To Martin Gannon, "it is the best way to cut into the culture.[6]"

8. To understand what "the Fatherland" is all about has little to do with[7] the aggressiveness* and rigidity* often attributed to Germans.[8] "What they really are is reflective of[9] a symphony."

potent [póutənt]: 강한, 강력한
anthropologist [ӕ̀nərəpɑ́lədʒist]: 인류학자
aggressiveness [əgrésivnis]: 공격성
rigidity [ridʒídəti]: 엄격성, 단단함

1) prove to be ~: ~이 되다 (turn out)
2) otherwise: 그렇지 않았더라면, 여기서는 quiet meals 가 아니었다면
3) mind-set: 사고(해석)방식
4) table of contents: 목차, 목록
5) credit A with B: B 를 A의 공으로 돌리다
6) cut into ~: ~에 파고들다
7) have little to do with ~: ~ 와 거의 관련이 없다
8) (which are) often attributed to Germans
be attributed to ~: ~ 에 기인하다, ~ 의 덕분으로 생각하다, ~ 을 특징짓다
9) be reflective of: reflect: 반영하다

Not only is music a cherished part of German character and history, but Mr. Gannon **contends*** that symphonic music symbolizes the dynamics of German society.[1] As in a symphony orchestra, **conformity*** is valued, order is important and rules are many, he says. And each person is expected to contribute fully his or her talents for the good of the whole.

9. The German education system further supports full participation by emphasizing **efficiency*** and preparation for a place in society for everyone.

10. "The German," Mr. Gannon said, "sees himself as an **integral*** part of society" and values combined effort. "If you approach German society that way, it is a lot easier" to understand.

11. Similarly, the French would prove far less frustrating to other cultures if approached[2] with the metaphor of "the French Vineyard" in mind, Mr. Gannon said. "France is a heavily agricultural country, much more so[3] than Germany or the United States," he noted. That rural element, combined with a Cartesian[4] educational system that emphasizes rational thought and mathematics, plants a perfectionist in the vineyard — a relationship reflected everywhere in France.

12. "You touch an apple in a shop in Paris and they get **annoyed*** because you are **violating*** the perfect picture they have developed there," Mr. Gannon said. Try to close a deal[5] with a French business executive you met only recently? Same reaction.

contend [kənténd]: 주장하다
conformity [kənfɔ́:rməti]: 순응, 적합, 일치
efficiency [ifíʃənsi]: 효율성, 능률
integral [íntigrəl]: 필수적인, 필요불가결한
annoy [ənɔ́i]: 짜증나게 하다, 약 오르게 하다
violate [váiəlèit]: 위반하다, 어기다

1) not only A but (also) B: A 뿐 아니라 B 이다
2) if (they are 생략) approached
3) much more so (= agricultural): 훨씬 더 그러한
4) Cartesian: 이성을 중시하는 Descartes 철학 [학파, 식]의
5) close a deal: 거래를 마무리하다

13. "The French want to know you, and they really won't deal with you until they get that," he said. "In the vineyard you nurture* relationships."

14. For Spanish society, the metaphor is the bullfight, "which really reflects Spanish culture, and is not a sport whatsoever,[1]" Mr. Gannon said. It is the proud individualism of the matador, the gang-like relationship of those in the bullring that reflects the personal relationship in Spain.

15. The Italian opera metaphor, he said, mirrors a society where "the drama is much more important than the individual and where emotions are so great that an individual can't hold them inside."

16. The American metaphor? Football, said Mr. Gannon. "Aggressiveness and individuality. In the United States, the society is individualistic and we focus on specialization. We try to learn something really well so we as an individual can do better than anyone we are competing with. Then there's huddling: What we're really good at[2] here is getting together on a problem, working intensely and then scattering."

nurture [nə́:rtʃə:r]: 양육하다, 보살피다

1) whatsoever: whatever 의 강조형
2) be good at ~: ~ 에 능숙하다, 잘하다

Section Three

Food & Culture

1. WHAT! No turkey?

Pat Dailey

1. Call it the raisin rebellion, a fateful day several years back, when Brian Bonebrake's family gathered around the Thanksgiving table, expecting that tradition would once again be the guiding force behind the meal.

2. Sure enough1), everything seemed just about as cheery and perfect as2) a Norman Rockwell painting3) until close examination revealed **shriveled*** black **specks*** in the **stuffing***. They might as well4) have been Japanese beetles.

3. "She put raisins in the bread stuffing! For a thousand years, my mother has made the exact same stuffing, and all of a sudden, she puts raisins in it. She's Sicilian. Sicilians don't do that," Bonebrake says, still undone5) by the case of stuffing bait-and-switch.6)

4. "She put them in because my stepfather wanted them. He was raised in Cuba and they eat stuff like that there," he adds. "And we had to get him an armchair. We always had side chairs around the table."

shrivel [ʃríːvəl]: 쪼글쪼글해지다
speck [spek]: 작은 얼룩, 작은 알갱이
stuffing [stʌ́fiŋ]: (만두 등과 같은 요리 속에 넣는) 소

---

1) sure enough : 틀림없이
2) seemed just about as ~ as —: 거의 꼭 — 처럼 ~ 여겨졌다
3) Norman Rockwell (1894-1978): a most renowned 20th century American painter and illustrator
4) might as well — : — 하는 편이 좋다, — 해도 나쁘지 않다
5) undone : undo의 p.p.
6) bait-and-switch : a misleading advertisement: 미끼상술

5. Thanksgiving, like most holidays, is all about ritual and sameness — the same turkey, the same stuffing, the same sweet potatoes. A new person or new recipe* thrown[1] into the mix can cause emotional rumblings* far greater than the stomach distress that follows the ritual overdose of turkey and pumpkin pie.

6. Just as the Boston Tea Party wasn't about orange pekoe, Bonebrake's dinner-table insurrection* probably had little to do with the offending raisins.[2] Food is invested with so many layers of emotional significance[3] that it often provokes responses[4] that aren't even remotely connected to nutrition* or taste.

7. "Holiday associations* are so strong, they're practically part of our DNA," says Ronna Kabatznick, a social psychologist from Berkeley, Calif. "When someone throws a curve,[5] whether it's different food, location or people, it completely uproots* our sense of realty. You end up looking[6] around and asking yourself, 'Is this really Thanksgiving?'"

8. Reality, on this particular day, is dished up on a big platter* and a battalion* of serving bowls. For many, a meal that's unfailingly consistent with[7] their accrued* memories is the only one

recipe [résəpì:]: 조리법
rumbling [rʌ́mbliŋ]: 우르렁거리는 소리
insurrection [insərékʃən]: 반란 사태
nutrition [nju:tríʃən]: 영양; 영양 섭취
association [əsòusiéiʃən]: 연합, 합동, (종종 pl.) 연상(聯想)
uproot [ʌprú:t]: (나무 · 화초 등을) 뿌리째 뽑다
platter [plǽtər] : (음식을 차려 내는 데 쓰는 큰 서빙용) 접시
battalion [bətǽljən]: 대대(大隊), 부대
accrue [əkrú:]: (금전 · 부채를) 누적하다, 축적하다

1) thrown : throw의 p.p. 앞의 recipe를 꾸며줌
2) have little to do with —: —와 거의 무관하다
3) be invested with —: —으로 싸이다 cf.) a town invested with fog: 안개에 싸인 도시
4) so ~ that —: 너무나 ~ 해서 — 하다
5) throw a curve: change unexpectedly and cause confusion
6) end up ~ing : 결국 ~하다
7) be consistent with ~: ~ 와 일치하다

worth having.[1] And it probably has less to do with feeling a special **kinship*** to everyone from the Pilgrims on down than it does with the comfort of familiarity.[2]

9. "Food mirrors all of our attachments to people and events," Kabatznick says. "We really don't want any of that to change, especially at the holidays."

10. "My mother could put my (Thanksgiving) dinner on a plate right now," says Allan Van Every, a Chicago physical therapist.[3] "I eat the same thing every year and I don't want it messed around with.[4] Matter of fact,[5] I know everything — the time we'll sit down, who I'll sit next to, even the exact plate she'll serve it on."

Creamed peas and onions

11. Elizabeth Barrett, a public relations executive, is so **adamant*** about having creamed peas and onions for Thanksgiving that she brings them along, no matter where she goes for dinner.

12. "I lived in Texas for eight years and where I went, so did they.[6] It came to be understood that if I was there, so were the peas. Then it was OK that I wasn't with my family as long as[7] I had my vegetables," she says. "I've been eating them since I was 2 years old. They define Thanksgiving."

13. Not everyone develops[8] the same **attachments***, of course, even

kinship [kínʃip]: 친족, 연대감, 동류의식
adamant [ǽdəmənt]: 요지부동의, 단호한
attachment [ətǽtʃmənt]: 애착, 믿음, 지지

1) worth ~ ing: ~ 할 만한 가치 있는
2) have less to do with A than B: B보다 A와 덜 관계가 있다 (B와 더 관련있다는 뜻)
3) physical therapist: 물리치료사
4) mess around with: create disorder: 마구 다루다, 망치다
5) (as a) matter of fact: 실상
6) they: peas and onions
7) as long as ~: ~ 하는 한
8) Not everyone develops = Everyone does not develop (Not 을 앞으로 두어 강조)

within families. While creamed peas are Thanksgiving's big sine qua non* for Barrett, the rest of her family's appetites* reside elsewhere. Now back in Chicago, she makes a few predictions* about what will be dished up to whom.

14. "Basically, my whole family eats a one-course dinner. No one else has anything to do with the peas and onions, so they're all mine. My brother insists on oyster stuffing, my sister eats sweet potatoes with icky[1] mini-marshmallows all over the top. Dad wants pumpkin pie with raisins and a whole can of Redi-Whip. That's so gross. We tell him, 'If you want it, Dad, bring it.' And he does. We accept each other's idiosyncrasies*. At least when it comes to[2] food."

15. Turkey unites them to some extent,[3] though. Barrett recalls the time a hapless guest proudly presented her contribution to dinner, a crown roast of pork.

16. "It was beautiful sitting there alongside the turkey, but we just stared at it like it was some alien life form. No one touched it. It was so sad. Pork with stuffing and cranberries? No way.[4]"

17. Save for[5] an occasional* ham or wayward* beef roast, a big, bronzed turkey is Thanksgiving's poster child,[6] and 90 percent of Americans will gobble the big bird today. The matter of stuffing, or dressing, is more contentious*.

sine qua non [sáini-kwei-nɑ́n]: L.) an indispensable condition: 필요불가결의 것, 필수조건
appetite [ǽpitàit]: 식욕
prediction [pridíkʃən]: 예측, 예견
idiosyncrasy [ìdiəsíŋkrəsi]: 특이한 성격, 별스러운 점
occasional [əkéiʒənəl]: 가끔의, 이따끔
wayward [wéiwə:rd]: 다루기 힘든, 변덕스러운
contentious [kənténʃəs]: 논쟁을 초래할 (듯한)

1) icky: (미국속어) 끈적끈적한, 불쾌한
2) when it comes to ~: concerning ~
3) to some extent: 어느 정도까지, 다소
4) no way: 말도 안 돼
5) save for ~: except ~: ~ 을 제외하고
6) poster child: a person or thing representing a particular quality or activity (특정 자질 · 활동을 나타내는) 전형으로 여겨지는 인물

18. One man, who asked that his name not be used, says that in retrospect*, last year's stuffing, although it signaled the end of a relationship, left him with much to be thankful for.

19. "It kind of[1] woke me up. The whole time we went out, six years, we created our own holidays, built up all these things that were important, that you come to expect and depend on. Last year, I'm carving the turkey, digging out the stuffing. The sausage and bread stuffing we always had was replaced* with cranberry rice stuffing—no warning.

20. It sounds simplistic, but I knew something a lot bigger than the stuffing wasn't right."

That's how mom did it

21. In social contexts*, food becomes a code with complex messages that speak volumes[2] about the status* of relationships. It may look as simple as a bowl of bread stuffing or cranberry relish, but it can harbor[3] a complex stew of emotions, starting with the age-old aphorism* that "food is love."

22. Katherine Lauderdale, who spent last Thanksgiving at a good friend's home, says the stuffing spat that ensued* all boiled down to[4] one thing.

retrospect [rétrəspèkt]: 회고하다
replace [ripléis]: 대신하다
context [kάntekst]: 맥락, 전후 사정
status [stéitəs]: 신분, 자격
aphorism [ǽfərìzəm]: 경구(警句)
ensue [ensúː]: 뒤따르다

1) kind of: sort of: 얼마쯤, 좀
2) speak volumes: say a great deal, reveal much
3) harbor: 마음에 품다
4) boil down to ~: mean, leaving out unnecessary elements: (구어) 결국 ~이 되다 요컨대 ~이 되다

23. "I was right, she was wrong," she says with unwavering certainty and nearly uncontrolled laughter, recalling that two adults spent the better part of[1] an hour scrapping over[2] white bread in the stuffing. The host thought more cornbread was called for[3] and proceeded to bake a pan of it to drive home her point.[4]

24. "I wouldn't call it screaming but we were making our points pretty aggressively. We cleared out[5] the kitchen. Pretty soon, everyone else was huddled* in the garage, trying to disappear," Lauderdale, a lawyer, recalls. "No one else wanted to have to take sides.[6]"

25. The issue was simple: One memory bumping up against another.

26. "It goes back to the way mothers make things. And my mother's is the right way," Lauderdale says, adding that she lost the battle and watched helplessly while her mother's beloved stuffing recipe was debauched*.

27. "I didn't kvetch* at the table or anything, but I made it perfectly clear that the stuff we ate was not my mother's recipe and that I had nothing to do with it,[7]" she says. "And by the way, I'm going back to my mother's this year."

28. Not everyone lives by such ironclad* rules. Bryan Coomes, a Paris-based photographer, has learned to endure, even appreciate change, even if it means roast turkey thighs for overseas celebrations*.

huddle [hʌ́dl]: 옹송그리며 모이다, 옹기종기 모여 있는 것
debauched [dibɔ́:tʃt]: ruined, debased / kvetch [kvetʃ]: 늘 불평만 하다, 투덜거리다
ironclad [-klæ̀d]: 깨뜨릴 수 없는, 엄격한 / celebration [sèləbréiʃən]: 기념, 축하

1) the better part of ~: ~ 의 대부분
2) scrap over ~: quarrel over ~
3) called for: needed
4) drive home a point: argue forcefully
5) clear out: (구어) 갑자기 떠나다.
6) take sides: (토론 등에서) 편을 들다
7) have nothing to do with ~: ~ 와 아무 관련 없다

29. "In France, the only time you find whole turkeys is Christmas. Otherwise, they sell these big legs with thigh attached so we put those frilly* papers on the end to make it seem festive*."

30. Even turkey has flown the coop[1] in some celebrations. Tim Hunt, a police officer assigned* to the bicycle patrol unit, says that as long as he's with family, he doesn't miss that most sacred* symbol a bit.

31. "I'm a vegetarian, so no more turkey, no more anything. My family has learned to be flexible*," he says. This year, he'll probably spring hommous and vegetarian fajitas, made with seitan (a type of wheat meat), on his family.

32. "They're pretty flexible, at least when I'm there to defend myself. But I'm always a little suspicious* that my dad grumbles* about the food just as soon as I've walked out that door."

33. Kabatznick reminds that the true spirit of Thanksgiving isn't found in a plate of creamed peas and onions or Sicilian stuffing.

34. "We're the envy of everyone on the planet. Instead of getting all caught up in[2] the horror of something that's different from your expectations, take it in stride.[3] Just be grateful you're lucky enough to have a nice hot meal and a warm place to eat it."

frilly [fríli]: 주름장식이 많은
festive [féstiv]: 축제의, 기념일의, 축하하는
assign [əsáin]: 맡기다, 배정하다
sacred [séikrid]: 성스러운, 종교적인
flexible [fléksəbəl]: 신축성 [융통성]있는
suspicious [səspíʃəs]: 의혹을 갖는, 수상쩍어 하는
grumble [grʌ́mbəl]: 투덜거리다, 불만 사항

1) flown the coop: run away
2) get all caught up in ~: get involved in ~: ~ 에 사로잡히다
3) take ~ in stride: actcept and deal with ~ easily: ~ 을 쉽게 뛰어넘다, (어려운 일을) 무난히 해결해 나가다

2. Food for Luck: New Year's Rituals

Dena Kleiman

1. The notion of eating foods to change one's fortune dates to ancient Babylonia and the world's first known recipes*, according to Nan Rothschild, professor of anthropology* at Barnard College.

2. "To say that a food brings good luck is a way of controlling the environment and one's destiny," Rothchild said.

3. It is especially at the beginning of each new year that[1] many societies rely on certain foods that are thought to possess magical powers. In the southern United States, for example, one popular New Year's dish is a casserole of rice and black-eyed peas known as Hoppin' John, a name of unknown origin.

4. The dish is said to bring prosperity* although few are sure why. Some theorize that a little of this concoction* goes a long way[2] and that those who eat it on New Year's Day will not go hungry.

5. In Italy, many people make a ritual* out of eating lentils. In Greece, families bake a special bread, vasilopita, and bury a coin inside it. "Whoever finds the coin will be wealthy," explains Diane Kochilas, author of "The Food and Wine of Greece" (St. Martin's Press).

recipe [résəpìː]: 조리법, 요리법
anthropology [æ̀nərəpάlədʒi]: 인류학
prosperity [prɑspérəti]: 번영, 번성, 번창
concoction [kɑnkάkʃən]: 혼합물
ritual [rítʃu-əl]: 의식 절차, 의례, 의식상의, 의식을 위한

1) it is ~ that: ~ 의 내용을 강조하는 it ~ that 용법
2) go a long way: (배고프지 않고) 오래 간다

6. In Japan, people eat long noodles. In Spain, the custom is to eat 12 individual grapes in the seconds leading up to the New Year. In India, revelers* eat fudge.

7. What ties these New Year's talismans* together is the seemingly universal notion that what one does and what one eats during those first delicate hours of the New Year will determine everything that will follow.

8. "It is as if we are reborn with the New Year and that whatever you do on that first day will affect what you do the rest of the year," said Jack Santino, a professor of folklore* and popular culture at Bowling Green University in Ohio.

9. Santino said that in Bowling Green, a rural community where families are largely of German descent*, the New Year's tradition is sauerkraut and pork. Pork is eaten, according to some folklorists, because pigs do not "scratch" the earth the way chickens do and anyone who eats pork on New Year's Day will not have to scratch for a living[1] in the coming year.

10. "You want to get off to a good start,[2]" said Frances Cattermole-Tally, executive editor of the Encyclopedia of American Popular Belief and Superstition, the first volume of which is to be published early next year by the University of California Press.

11. According to the volume, Americans welcome the New Year with a wide panoply* of good luck foods, including cabbage, herring, honey, sardines and salt.

reveler [rév-ələr]: (보통 다른 사람들과 술을 마시며) 흥청거리는 사람
talisman [tǽlismən]: 부적, 불가사의한 힘이 있는 것
folklore [fóuklɔ̀ːr]: 민속, 전통문화
descent [disént]: 가계, 혈통, 출신.
panoply [pǽnəpli]: 모음, 집합

1) scratch for a living: work hard for the money needed to live on
2) get off to a good start: begin well

12. The truth is that many of these culinary* traditions are rooted in a simplistic rationale* and the primitive notion that by putting a concept symbolically in one's mouth, one literally can embody it.

13. "You eat it; you swallow it; it becomes part of yourself," explained Barbara Kirshenblatt-Gimblett, an anthropologist and folklorist who is chairman of the Department of Performance Studies at New York University.

14. The symbols, too, are simplistic and their aspirations[1] downright self-centered. Rather than addressing larger societal concerns like world peace and the benefit of mankind, they revolve around selfish wishes like personal gain, abundance*, fertility*, and health.

15. Cattermole-Tally says, for example, that many Americans eat herring for the New Year because herring swim in such large numbers that they are a symbol of abundance.[2] Eat a herring, the logic goes, and abundance will be yours in the new year.

16. In fact, fish are a favorite New Year's fare, Cattermole-Tally said because they swim forward and the belief is that people who eat fish will get ahead[3] in the new year, too.

17. "So far[4] it's worked for me," said Martha Henning, 77, a retired secretary in Washington Township, New Jersey, who has been eating herring every New Year's Eve since she was a young bride in 1934. "I've had a pretty lucky life."

18. William H. Wiggins, a professor of African American studies at Indiana University who is the author of "Oh Freedom!: Afro-American Emancipation* Celebrations," (University of Tennessee)

culinary [kʌ́lənèri]: 요리의, 음식의
rationale [ræ̀ʃənǽl]: 이유, 근거 / abundance [əbʌ́ndəns]: 풍부
fertility [fəːrtíləti]: 비옥함, 생식력 / emancipation [imæ̀nsəpéiʃən]: (노예) 해방

1) aspirations (are 생략)
2) such ~ that —: 너무나 ~ 해서 — 이다
3) get ahead: be successful
4) so far: 지금까지는

says that collard greens and cabbage are good luck foods because they are green and resemble money.

19. The quest for money in the new year is also seen in Italian customs. If Italians are not eating lentils, says Carol Field, author of "Celebrating Italy" (William Morrow), they are eating chiacchiere, pieces of dough that look like lentils and are drizzled with honey, so that the New Year will not only be prosperous but sweet.

20. In Piedmont, luck finds its vessel in risotto topped with melted fontina because it is a symbol of fertility.

21. "If you're really lucky, you get shavings of white truffles," Field points out.

22. In Rome, friends exchange dried figs soaked in honey. In southern Italy they prepare a lusty* Sicilian creation that is a lasagna packed with[1] ricotta cheese and topped with a dark tomato ragu.

23. Puns* play an important role[2] in the good luck foods of China and Japan. In Chinese, for example, the word yu means fish. Its homonym* means surplus* and abundance. Fish is therefore the omen* of choice for the new year, which starts on Feb. 15, according to Charlie Chin, community education director of the New York Chinatown History Project.

24. Similarly, in Japan, according to Elizabeth Andoh, author of "An Ocean of Flavor: The Japanese Way with Fish and Seafood," (William Morrow), black beans are a food for the new year because they symbolize hard work and diligence.

lusty [lʌ́sti]: 풍부한, 푸짐한
pun [pʌn]: 말장난, 말재간, 말장난을 하다
homonym [hámənìm]: 동철이의어, 동음이의어
surplus [sə́:rplʌs]: 과잉, 과잉의, 잉여의
omen [óumən]: 징조, 조짐

1) packed with ~: ~로 꽉 채우다
2) play a role: 역할을 하다

25. Another popular New Year's custom in Japan, where at the stroke* of midnight the temple bells ring 108 times to rid the world of evil,[1] is eating toshi koshi soba, or year-end noodles.

26. These extremely long noodles are sucked into the mouth. They should not be cut on the theory that the longer the noodles, the longer and better[2] the New Year.

27. In Ireland, the Celtic new year, traditionally Nov. 1, is often celebrated with a cake known as barn brack. It is filled with little symbols, each said[3] to dictate* one's fortune for the coming year. Guests do not know which of the charms they might receive.

28. A ring, for example, might indicate an impending* marriage. A button, bachelorhood. A rag might predict poverty; a thimble, spinsterhood*; a coin, wealth.

29. "In Ireland it's not so much good luck as what kind of luck might be out there,[4]" said Malachy McCormick, author of "Irish Country Cooking," (Clarkson Potter). He said his mother always prepared such a cake in his youth.

30. In India, the New Year celebrations at the end of October, the first and the middle of January focus on no one food but rather a balance of flavors, according to Julie Sahni, author of "Classic Indian Cooking," (Morrow).

31. Appam, a traditional cake made with rice flour, coconut, milk, and a kind of palm sap, is served along with[5] a fudge called barfi. Both symbolize the wish for life to be sweet. But Sahni said other dishes, like mulligatawny soup (said to be good for a hangover) and green mango chutney, which is both sweet and

stroke [strouk]: 타격, 치는 소리(시계·종 따위)
dictate [díkteit]: 받아쓰게 하다, 명령하다, 지시하다
impending [impéndiŋ]: 곧 닥칠, 임박한
spinsterhood [spínstəːrdhùd]: 독신

1) rid A of B: A 에게서 B 를 제거하다
2) the ~er, the —-er: ~하면 할수록, 더 —-하다
3) each (is 생략) said
4) not so much A as B: A 라기보다는 B 이다
5) along with ~: ~ 와 함께, ~ 에 더하여.

hot, are served as well[1] because a New Year's feast must include tastes that are at once sweet, savory, sour and hot.[2]

32. "The idea is to serve something that brings many flavors in your mouth, with the hope that life is going to bring many elements of pleasure and pain and you should take it all in good spirit," Sahni said.

1) as well: 또한, 게다가
2) at once A and B: A 이기도 하고 B 이기도 한

Section Four

Education

1. New Under the Tree: Computers for Tots*

Carol Lawson

1. Diane Bishop looked tense. And confused.

2. There she was, in the midst of the Christmas rush, surrounded by the electronic beeps, clicks and flashing lights of the Learning Center on the second floor at F.A.O. Schwarz.

3. She was picking out[1] a present for her daughter, Amanda. Actually, Ms. Bishop was in the famous toy store to select more than a present.

4. "You could call it a milestone*," she said. "It will be right up there in Amanda's life with her first tooth, first bicycle and first airplane ride."

5. She was in the Learning Center to pick out Amanda's first computer.

6. Amanda is 2 years old. Like many children her age who can barely pronounce the word computer, she will wake up to find[2] one[3] under the tree Monday morning.

7. Computer makers are plugging into[4] new territory*. First they

tot [tɑt]: 어린아이, 꼬마
milestone [máilstòun]: 중요한 단계, 획기적인 사건
territory [térətɔ̀:ri]: 지역, 영토

1) pick out: choose
2) wake up to find: wake up and find (to 부정사의 결과적 용법)
3) one: a computer
4) plug into: (전기 기구)의 플러그를 끼우다, 접속하다

took on[1] the office. Then they wired the home and the classroom. Now they are going after[2] the playroom.

8. When Amanda Bishop was born, computers for preschoolers were barely a blip on the brain waves[3] of computer designers. But all that has changed rapidly as computer manufacturers tuned into[4] the anxieties of parents who want to program very young children for the path to Princeton.

9. Computers for preschoolers are essentially video games with an educational twist.[5] They are designed to grab the attention of[6] young minds with peppy[7] electronic music and animated figures that look cute and move fast.

10. For example, press the letter S on the Fisher-Price Spelling Starter, and a spider dances on the screen. Or press the number 4 on the Fisher-Price Math Starter, and four joggers spring across the screen.

11. The computers, which range in price from $20 to $200, feature programs that teach such rudimentary* "subjects" as shapes, colors, numbers and letters. There also are more advanced programs that aim to teach spelling, reading, vocabulary and math.

12. "The goal is to prepare children for school and help them do better in the classroom," said Jon Campbell, media relations manager for Texas Instruments Inc., which this year added four new preschool computers to what it calls its EET line, or electronic educational toys.

13. Another goal is to help children make friends with computers. "They are going to live with computers their whole lives," Mr. Campbell said.

rudimentary [rú:dəməntri]: 가장 기본(기초)적인

1) take on: 공략하다, 떠맡다
2) go after ~: pursue: ~의 획득에 노력하다; (여자 등)의 뒤를 좇아다니다
3) barely a blip on the brain waves: hardly a thought in the mind
4) tuned into: alert to
5) twist: unexpected characteristic: 예기치 않은, 뜻밖의 전개
6) grab the attention of: gain the interest of
7) peppy: lively

14. "The future for these products looks very good," he said. "There is a growing emphasis on education, and parents and grandparents want to see their children get ahead.[1]"

15. The expanding preschool market includes electronic toys that, with their keyboards and display screens, look like miniature* personal computers. There also is an array* of educational software that can be used with the parents' more sophisticated* home computer.

16. The products come in boxes with the word "educational" stamped on them. They are packaged with the promise of being "easy to use," "friendly," and "fun."

17. Fisher-Price's software that "teaches number recognition" to children as young as 3, comes with the message: "No previous computer experience necessary."

18. Subjects are taught through the presentation of questions or problems. Children register their answers by pushing a button.

19. The makers of this merchandise endorse* the theory of child-rearing that says youngsters learn by positive reinforcement.[2] Right answers are usually greeted with a burst of upbeat electronic fanfare*.

20. The Socrates Touch Pad signals correct responses with an applauding robot. Texas Instruments' Speak and Read talks back, exclaiming*, "You're right! Great!"

21. Wrong answers elicit* an electronic dirge* or an empathetic* voice that says, "Wrong answer. Try again."

miniature [míniətʃər]: 모형, 축소형
array [əréi]: 집합체, 모음, 배열하다, 진열하다
sophisticated [səfístəkèitid]: 세련된, 교양 있는
endorse [endɔ́:rs]: 지지하다, 승인하다, 찬성하다
fanfare [fǽnfɛər]: 팡파르 / exclaim [ikskléim]: 소리치다, 외치다
elicit [ilísit]: (진리·사실 따위를) 이끌어 내다, 유도해 내다.
dirge [də:rdʒ]: 만가 / empathetic [èmpəθétik]: 강한, 단호한

1) get ahead: succeed
2) positive reinforcement: 긍정적 강화 (격려, 칭찬 등)

22. Some experts take a dim view of[1] encouraging very young children to learn with computers. They say that parents and other adults, not to mention[2] old-fashioned books, can do the job just as well.[3]

23. Ms. Bishop would not hear of it. "My daughter is applying to nursery school," she said. "Maybe this will give her an edge.[4]" After nearly two hours of pushing buttons and trying to become computer-literate on the preschool level, Ms. Bishop made her choice.

24. For $45 she bought My Little Computer, made by Texas Instruments. Designed for children aged 2 to 6, it has simple programs that teach matching skills and multiple choice as well as more advanced programs for learning numbers, letters, spelling, counting and names of animals.

25. Some educators say that though preschoolers might have fun with these computers, they do not necessarily[5] learn from them. Another **objection*** is the introduction of academic stress so early in life.

26. "We have to recognize that computers are a fact of life, but I am concerned that these toys are putting too much pressure on children at too young an age," said Barbara A. Willer, a former preschool teacher and the public affairs director of the National Association for the Education of Young Children.

27. "There is an overemphasis on the memorization of letters and numbers," she said. "Parents think they are **precursors*** of later learning, of higher scores. But children who are not ready

objection [əbdʒékʃən]: 이의, 반대
precursor [prikə́:rsər]: 선도자

1) take a dim view of: look on negatively
2) not to mention ~:~은 언급할 필요도 없고, 물론이고
3) as well: 마찬가지로 잘
4) edge: advantage
give an edge: help to gain an advantage
5) not necessarily ~: 반드시 ~ 하는 건 아니다

to gain those skills may become turned off to[1] learning or convinced they are dumb."

1) turned off to ~: no longer interested in ~

2. For Japanese, Cramming for Exams Starts Where the Cradle Leaves Off[1)]

Steven R. Weisman

1. Tokyo — Like many Japanese, Naoto Eguchi feels relentless* pressure to get ahead.[2)] Rising at dawn, he works a full day with his regular colleagues* and another three hours each evening in special study sessions. He then does a couple of hours of work at home before going to bed at midnight.

2. It is a heavy burden for an 11-year-old.

3. Naoto's immediate goal is to pass the entrance examinations for a private junior high school, a crucial* step for eventual admission to a prestigious* university. But he is already thinking about the future.

4. "My goal is to get a good job with a good company," he said.

5. The struggle to succeed in one of the world's most competitive societies is starting earlier and earlier, and nowhere is it more evident than in the growing popularity* of cram schools that train students for examinations for private schools and colleges.

relentless [riléntlis]: 끈질긴, 가차 없는
colleague [kάli:g]: (같은 직장이나 직종에 종사하는) 동료
crucial [krú:ʃəl]: 중대한, 결정적인
prestigious [prestídʒiəs]: 명망 있는, 일류의
popularity [pὰpjəlǽrəti]: 인기

---

1) leave off: stop
2) get ahead: succeed

6. Once on the fringe* of the system, cram* schools, or jukus, are so pervasive* and time-consuming in Japan that, especially for the elite, they have begun to function as a kind of shadow educational system, supplanting* regular schools in importance for parents and students and reaching down to 2 and 3-year-old children.

7. The rise of jukus is praised as one of the secrets of Japanese success, a healthy reflection of a system of advancement based on merit*. It is also criticized* as a movement forcing a new generation to surrender* its childhood out of an obsession* with status and getting ahead.

8. "Jukus are harmful to Japanese education and to children," said Ikuo Amano, professor of sociology at the University of Tokyo. "It's not healthy for kids to have so little free time. It is not healthy to become completely caught up in[1] competition and status at such a young age."

9. Recently, the Yano Research Institute found that nearly 4.4 million students enrolled in some 50,000 to 60,000 jukus. That represents 18.6 percent of elementary school children and 52.2 percent of students in seventh through ninth grades. Japanese spent $10.9 billion on tutoring and cram schools last year, according to the institute, including $9 billion on jukus for students in the ninth grade or below—almost double the figure spent seven years ago.

10. The people who run and teach at jukus say the schools are popular only because they work, creating a lively and interesting environment in which students learn because they are enjoying themselves.

fringe [frindʒ]: 가장자리, 외변
cram [kræm]: 밀어 [쑤셔]넣다, 벼락치기 공부를 하다, cram school: 주입식 과외학원
pervasive [pərvéisiv]: 만연하는, (구석구석) 스며드는 / supplant [səplǽnt]: 대신하다
merit [mérit]:가치 있는 요소, 장점 / criticize [krítisàiz]: 비평하다, 비판하다
surrender [səréndər]: 항복(하다), 포기하다 / obsession [əbséʃən]: 집착, 강박 관념

1) becomne caught up in = get very involved in

11. One of the most prestigious cram schools for 2-and 3-year-olds, Shingakai Juky, sends most of its prekindergarten graduates to prestigious elementary schools. If these students get good grades in a prestigious school, they can advance all the way to a university without having to take examinations.

12. "We really don't push knowledge on them," said Kigen Jujimoto, head of a branch of this juku in northwest Tokyo. "We are interested in teaching them how to play and enjoy learning."

13. In a nearby class, eight children, each about 3, sat politely in little chairs in a row as a teacher held up pictures of a kite, a dragon, and other objects, calling on the students to identify them. "What is this shape?" she then said, holding up first a square, a triangle, and then a circle.

14. Several mothers who were waiting to pick up their children, expressed anxiety about subjecting their youngsters to such pressure. But they reasoned that it would be worth it if their children got into private schools early and did not have to worry about passing examinations later on.

15. "It's not an ideal thing to send your kids to such a place," said one mother, asking not to be identified for fear of criticism from other parents. She said she thought that her daughter was having a good time in this school, but continued, "If I told you I wasn't thinking about entrance examinations, I would be lying."

16. Juku teachers and administrators say that because their schools are profit-making enterprises, they have to guarantee results to succeed. The results are easy to measure, because they depend on how many graduates pass the examinations for private school.

17. The "examination hell" inflicted[1] on children is widely criticized in Japan. In a recent survey, two-thirds of parents said competitive examinations were their worst problem in raising children. But parents are also eager to give their children every advantage.

---

1) inflict [inflíkt]: (타격·고통 따위를) 주다, 가하다(on)

18. "Jukus are playing on the status anxieties of these parents," said Makoto Oda, an author who taught in jukus in Tokyo for more than 20 years. "All parents are absolutely terrified that their children will fall behind."

19. Juku defenders say that students are only gaining the discipline* and ability to withstand* pressure that they will need in life.

20. But the very success of jukus in training youngsters to pass exams has made the competition worse: jukus help more students pass exams, so the exams have to be made more difficult.

21. "Jukus are raising a generation of kids who can only pass entrance examinations," said Hiroyuki Tsukamoto, an official of the Japan Teachers Union. "But the most important educational purpose is giving children the ability to live in society That's being left out."1)

22. The Education Ministry has tried to combat the juku system by improving public schools, reducing class sizes, upgrading teacher training, and making the curriculum* more flexible. But ministry officials acknowledge that those steps have not worked.

discipline [dísəplin]: 규율, 훈육
withstand [wiðstǽnd]: 견뎌내다
curriculum [kəríkjələm]: 교육과정

1) left out : omitted, not included

Section Five

Nation & The World

1. Unhappy America

If America can learn from its problems, instead of blaming others, it will come back stronger

1. Nations, like people, occasionally get the blues;[1] and right now the United States, normally the world's most self-confident place, is glum*. Eight out of ten Americans think their country is heading in the wrong direction. The hapless George Bush is partly to blame for this: his approval* ratings* are now sub-Nixonian.[2] But many are concerned not so much about a failed president as about flailing* nation.

2. One source of angst* is the sorry state of American capitalism. The "Washington consensus*" told the world that open markets and deregulation* would solve its problems. Yet American house prices are falling faster than during the Depression, petrol is more expensive than in the 1970s, banks are collapsing*, the euro is kicking sand in the dollar's face,[3] credit is scarce, recession* and inflation both threaten the economy, consumer confidence is an oxymoron* and Belgians have just bought Budweiser, "America's beer".

glum [glʌm]: 침울한 / approval [əprú:vəl]: 인정, (특히 계획 · 요청에 대한) 승인
rating [réitiŋ]: 순위, 시청률, 청취율
flail [fleil]: (팔다리를) 마구 흔들다, 매타작을 하다
angst [ɑ:ŋkst]: (삶에 대한) 불안 / consensus [kənsénsəs]: 의견일치, 합의
deregulation [di:règjəléiʃən]: (무역 등에 대한) 규제 철폐
collapse [kəlǽps]: 붕괴되다, 무너지다 / recession [riséʃ-ən]: 불경기, 불황
oxymoron [ɑ̀ksimɔ́:rɑn]: 모순어법 (예: cruel kindness)

1) get the blues: 마음이 울적하다, 슬퍼지다
2) sub-Nixonian: President Nixon 보다 아래인
3) euro 가 dollar 에 정면으로 모래를 끼얹듯 가치가 올라가고 있다는 뜻

3. And it's not just the downturn* that has caused this discontent*. Many Americans feel as if they missed the boom. Between 2002 and 2006 the incomes of 99% rose by an average of 1% a year in real terms, while those of the top 1% rose by 11% a year; three-quarters of the economic gains during Mr Bush's presidency went to that top 1%. Economic envy, once seen as a European vice, is now rife*. The rich appear in Barack Obama's speeches not as entrepreneurial* role models but as modern versions of the "malefactors* of great wealth" denounced* by Teddy Roosevelt a century ago: this lot,[1] rather than building trusts, avoid taxes and ship jobs to Mexico. Globalisation is under fire:[2] free trade is less popular in the United States than in any other developed country, and a nation built on immigrants is building a fence to keep them out. People mutter about nation-building beginning at home: why, many wonder, should American children do worse at reading than Polish ones and at maths than Lithuanians?

The dragon's breath on your shoulder

4. Abroad, America has spent vast amounts of blood and treasure, to little purpose.[3] In Iraq, finding an acceptable exit will look like success; Afghanistan is slipping. America's claim to be a beacon of freedom in a dark world has been dimmed by

downturn [-́tə̀:rn]: (매출 등의) 감소; (경기) 하강
discontent [dìskəntént]: 불만
rife [raif]: 만연한
entrepreneur [ɑ̀:ntrəprənə́:r]: (특히 모험적인) 사업가 , ~ial
malefactor [mǽəfæ̀ktə:r]: 악인, 악한
denounce [dináuns]: 맹렬히 비난하다, 고발하다

1) lot: 제비뽑기, 추첨; 한 무더기; 한 떼, 사람들; 운명; 많음; (구어) 놈, 자식.
2) under fire: 비난을 받아
3) to little pupose: 별 소용없이

Guantanamo, Abu Ghraib and the flouting* of the Geneva Conventions amid the panicky* "unipolar" posturing* in the aftermath* of september 11th.

5. Now the world seems very multipolar. Europeans no longer worry about American ascendancy*. The French, some say, understood the Arab world rather better than the neoconservatives did. Russia, the Gulf Arabs and the rising powers of Asia scoff* openly at the Washington consensus, China in particular spooks* America — and may do so even more over the next few weeks of Olympic medal-gathering. Americans are discussing the rise of China and their consequent* relative decline; measuring when China's economy will be bigger and counting its missiles and submarines has become a popular pastime* in Washington. A few years ago, no politician would have been seen with a book called "the post-American world". Mr Obama has been conspicuously* reading Fareed Zakaria's recent volume.

6. America has got into funks* before now. In the 1950s it went into a Sputnik-driven[1)] spin* about Soviet power; in the 1970s there was Watergate, Vietnam and the oil shocks; in the late 1980s Japan seemed to be buying up America. Each time, the United States rebounded, because the country is good at fixing itself. Just as American capitalism allows companies to die, and

flout [flaut]: 비웃다, (법 등을 공공연히) 어기다
panic [pǽnik]: 돌연한 공포, 당황하(게 하)다, ~ky: 당황한, 공황상태의
posturing [pάstʃər]: 자세(를 취하다)
aftermath [-mæ̀θ]: (전쟁 · 사고 등의) 여파
ascendancy [əséndənsi]: 우세, 주도 [지배]권
scoff [skɔ:f]: 비웃다, 조롱하다 (at)
spook [spu:k]: 유령, 겁먹게 하다
consequent [kάnsikwènt]: ~의 결과로 일어나는
pastime [pǽstàim]: 취미, 오락
conspicuous [kənspíkjuəs]: 눈에 잘 띄는, 현저한
funk [fʌŋk]: 펑크(강한 비트의 음악); 두려움, 걱정
spin [spin]: 회전(하다); 현기증, 혼란

1) Sputnik: 러시아가 발사한 세계 최초의 인공위성 (1957년)

to be created, quickly, so its political system reacts fast.[1] In Europe, political leaders emerge slowly, through party hierarchies; in America, the primaries* permit inspirational unknowns to burst into the public consciousness from nowhere.

7. Still, countries, like people, behave dangerously when their mood turns dark. If America fails to distinguish between what it needs to change and what it needs to accept, it risks hurting not just allies and trading partner, but also itself.

The Asian scapegoat

8. There are certainly areas where change is needed. The credit crunch[2] is in part the consequence of a flawed* regulatory system. Lax* monetary policy allowed Americans to build up debts and fuelled a housing bubble that had to burst eventually. Lessons need to be learnt from both of those mistakes; as they do from widespread concerns about the state of education and health care. Over-unionised and unaccountable*, America's school system needs the same sort of competition that makes its universities the envy of the world. American health care, which manages to be the most expensive on the planet even though it fails properly to care for the tens of millions of people, badly[3] needs reform.

9. There have been plenty of mistakes abroad, too. Waging a war on terror was always going to be like pinning jelly to a wall. As for Guantanamo bay,[4] it is the most profoundly un-American place on the planet: rejoice when it is shut.

hierarchy [háiərà:rki]: 계급제도
primary [práimeri]: 주된, 주요한; 최초의; (미국에서) 예비 선거
flaw [flɔ:]: 결함, 흠, ~ed: 결함 있는 / lax [læks]: 느슨한, 해이한
unaccountable [ʌ̀nəkáuntəbəl]: 설명할 수 없는; 책임을 지지 않는

1) just as ~ , so ~: 꼭 ~ 처럼 ~하다
2) crunch: (경제의) 침체, 불황
3) badly: 대단히, 몹시 (greatly)
4) Guantanamo bay is a detainment facility of the United States located in Cuba.

10. In such areas America is already showing its genius for reinvention. Both the Republican and Democratic presidential candidates promise to close Guantanamo. As his second term ticks down, even Mr Bush has begun to see the limits of unilateralism*. Instead of just denouncing and threatening the "axis of evil" he is working more closely with allies (and non-allies) in Asia to calm down North Korea. For the first time he has just let American officials join in the negotiations* with Iran about its fishy[1] nuclear programme.

11. That America is beginning to correct its mistakes is good; and there's plenty more of that to be done. But one source of angst demands a change in attitude rather than a drive[2] to restore the status quo:[3] America's relative decline, especially compared with Asia in general and China in particular.[4]

12. The economic gap between America and a rising Asia has certainly narrowed; but worrying about it is wrong for two reasons. First, even at its present growth rate, China's GDP will take a quarter of a century to catch up with[5] America's; and the internal tensions that China's rapidly changing economy has caused may well[6] lead it to stumble before then. Second, even if Asia's rise continues unabated*, it is wrong – and profoundly unAmerican – to regard this as a problem. Economic growth, like trade, is not a zero-sum game.[7] The faster China and india grow, the more American goods they buy. And they are booming largely because they have adopted America's ideas. America

unilateralism [jù:nəlǽtərəlizəm]: 일방적 핵 폐기주의
negotiation [nigòuʃiéiʃən]: 협상, 교섭
abate [əbéit]: (강도가) 약해지다, 약화시키다, unabated: 약화 되지 않는

1) fishy: (구어) 의심스러운, 수상한
2) drive: 의욕, 추진력, 맹공격
3) status quo: 현상(現狀)
4) in general: 일반적으로, in particular: 특히
5) catch up with ~: ~ 를 따라잡다
6) may well ~: ~해도 좋다(허가); ~일지도 모른다(가능성)
7) zero-sum game: 한 쪽의 득점[이익]이 다른 쪽에 실점[손실]이 되어+-제로가 되는 게임

should regard their success as a tribute*, not a threat, and celebrate in it.

13. Many Americans, unfortunately, are unwilling to do so. Politicians seeking a scapegoat for America's self-made problems too often point the finger at[1] the growing power of once-poor countries, accusing them of[2] stealing American jobs and objecting when they try to buy American companies. But if America reacts by turning in on itself[3] – raising trade barriers and rejecting foreign investors – it risks exacerbating* the economic troubles that lie behind its current funk.

14. Everybody goes through bad times. Some learn from the problems they have caused themselves, and come back stronger. Some blame others, lash out[4] and damage themselves further. America has had the wisdom to take the first course many times before. Let's hope it does so again.

tribute [tríbjuːt]: 헌사, 경의
exacerbate [igzǽsərbèit, iksǽs-]: 악화시키다; 격분시키다.

1) point the finger at ~: ~을 비난[비판]하다, 책망하다
2) accuse A of B: B 의 일로 A 를 비난하다
3) turn in on itself: 자기 안으로만[본인의 문제에만]몰입하다
4) lash out: 강타하다; 폭언을 퍼붓다, 비난하다

2. Twenty Years after the Wall: So much gained, so much to lose

Over the past 20 years economic freedom has outpaced political liberty. Neither should be taken for granted.1)

1. "Of all places it was in divided Berlin in divided Germany in divided Europe that the cold war erupted* into an east-west street party," this newspaper observed 20 years ago. Even to those who had been confident of the eventual triumph of the West, the fall of the Berlin Wall was surprisingly accidental. When 200,000 East Germans took advantage of Hungary's decision to open its borders and fled to the West, their communist government decided to modify* the travel restrictions that imprisoned them. Asked about the timing,2) the unbriefed3) propaganda* minister mumbled: "As far as I know, effective immediately." When that was reported on television, the Berliners were off. Baffled* border guards who would have shot their "comrades" a week earlier let the crowd through – and a barrier that had divided the world was soon being gleefully dismantled*. West Germany's chancellor, Helmut Kohl, was so unready for history that he was out of the country.

erupt [irʌ́pt]: 분출하다, 발발하다. / modify [mɑ́dəfài]: 수정하다, 바꾸다
propaganda [prɑ̀pəgǽndə]: (주의·신념의) 선전
baffle [bǽfəl]: 좌절시키다, 당황케 하다.
dismantle [dismǽntl]: 분해하다, 해체하다

1) take ~ for granted: ~ 를 당연시하다
2) (As he was 생략) asked ~
3) unbriefed: briefing (상황설명, 행동 개시 전의 최종 협의) 을 받지 않은

2. The destruction of the Iron Curtain on November 9th 1989 is still the most remarkable political event of most people's lifetimes: it set free millions of individuals and it brought to an end[1] a global conflict that threatened nuclear **annihilation***. For liberals in the West, it still stands as a reminder both of what has been won since and what is still worth fighting for.

Remember the stasi,[2] but don't forget the fridges[3]

3. Yet the past two decades have seen economic freedom advance further than political freedom. Talk 20 years ago of a peaceful new world order has disappeared. New divisions have emerged out of nationalism, religion or just "fear of the other". Rather than making the case for democracy **unassailable***, plenty of countries, including, alas, a few of the old Warsaw Pact members,[4] most of the Arab world and China, have been able to run shamelessly repressive authoritarian **regimes***. When Western leaders visit Moscow, Riyadh or Beijing, they merely mumble about human rights. The **presumption*** has become that such regimes will endure.

4. By contrast, "globalization", that awkward term that covers the freer movement of goods, capital, people and ideas around the globe, has become the governing principle of commerce. That does not mean it is universally accepted: witness the **travails***

annihilation [ənàiəléiʃən]: 전멸, 절멸,
assail [əséil]: 공격하다, (비난·질문·요망 따위로) 공박하다, 비난하다
unassailable: 공격할 수 없는, 확고한
regime [reiʒí:m]: 정권, 체제
presumption [prizʌ́mpʃən]: 추정, 가정 travail [trəvéil]: 고생, 고역

1) bring to an end: 종식시키다, 끝내다
2) stasi: [G.]슈타지(옛 동독의 비밀경찰)
3) fridge: refrigerator
4) Warsaw Pact: 1955년 동유럽 8개국 (소비에트 연방, 폴란드, 체코슬로바키아, 동독, 헝가리, 루마니아, 불가리아, 알바니아) 이 바르샤바에 모여서 결성한 군사조약

of the Doha round of trade talks.[1] But few places openly oppose it. In the economic sphere, illiberalism[2] usually has to disguise itself through governments trying to adapt it, stressing "capitalism with Chinese characteristics", "stakeholder[3] capitalism", "fair trade" and so on.[4] Even after the crunch,[5] the commercial classes assume that the world will become more **integrated***: who can resist economic logic and technology?*

5. It is not hard to see why such a presumption should exist. Consider two successes of economic liberalism, both somewhat under-appreciated at the moment. The first is its role 20 years ago. The East Berliners rushing to the West were not just fleeing the Stasi; they also came in search of fridges, jeans and Coca-Cola from supermarkets. By then communism, for all[6] its tanks and missiles, was plainly a less efficient economic machine. Mikhail Gorbachev deserves credit for[7] allowing so many serfs to escape so peacefully; but the Soviet Union **crumbled*** because it could not produce the goods.

6. And even if the current round of globalisation technically began before the wall fell, it was spurred on[8] by it. (The word seldom appeared in The Economist before 1986 and began to be common only in the 1990s.) Globalisation would have meant much less if half of Europe had been bricked in;[9] many instinctively statist giants of the emerging world, such as Brazil,

integrate [íntəgrèit]: 통합하다
crumble [krʌ́mbl]: 바스러지다, 허물어지다

---

1) Doha round: 2001년 선진국들이 개발도상국들의 경제발전을 돕자는 의도에서 카타르의 수도 도하에서 출범
2) illiberalism : 반자유주의
3) stakeholder: 내깃돈을 맡(아 보관하)는 제삼자, 판돈보관인
4) and so on: 기타 등등
5) crunch : (경제의) 침체, 불황
6) for all ~ : in spite of ~
7) deserve credit for ~: ~ 에 대한 평가 받을 자격이 있다
8) spur on: 박차를 가하다
9) 'Berlin Wall 이 가로막았더라면' 의 뜻

India or even China, would have been far slower to open up their economies if a semi-credible **alternative*** had still existed.

7. That points to the second under-appreciated success. At present capitalism is too often judged by the **excesses*** of a few bankers. But when historians come to write about the past quarter-century,[1] Lehman Brothers and Sir Fred "the Shred" Goodwin will account for[2] fewer pages than the 500m people dragged out of absolute poverty into something resembling the middle class. Their success is not just a wonderful thing in itself—the greatest leap forward in economic history. It has also helped spur on other chaotic freedoms: look at the way ideas, good, bad and mad, are texted around the world.

8. For in the end, no matter what China's leaders tell Mr Obama when he visits Beijing later this month, economic and political liberty are linked—not as tightly as people hoped 20 years ago, but still linked. Look forward, and China's internet-obsessed emerging middle class will surely have an **appetite*** for liberty beyond the purely economic. Change could happen as unexpectedly as it did in 1989. Even the most fearsome **fortresses*** of **repression*** can eventually be **breached***. Then it was Honecker and Ceausescu; tomorrow it might be Castro, Ahmadinejad or Mugabe; one day Chavez or even Hu.

alternative [ɔːltə́ːrnətiv]: 대안, 대체 가능한 (것)
excess [iksés]: 과도, 과잉
appetite [ǽpItàit]: 식욕, 욕구
fortress [fɔ́ːrtris]: 요새
repression [ripréʃ-ən]: 탄압, 억압
breach [briːtʃ]: 깨뜨리다; (법률·약속)을 어기다

1) the passed quarter-century: 지난 25년
2) account for ~: 책임을 지다, 떠맡다

Marx to market

9. Put another way,[1)] the presumption that political freedom will never catch up with[2)] economic freedom could turn out to be joyously wrong. The problem is that this gap could also be closed another way. Economic freedom could be slowed down, perhaps even reversed*, by politics.

10. For Western liberals, even ones who believe in open markets as unreservedly[3)] as this paper, that means facing up to[4)] some hard facts about the popularity of their creed. Western capitalism's victory over its rotten communist rival does not ensure it an enduring franchise* from voters. As Karl Marx pointed out during globalization's last great surge* forward in the 19th century, the magic of comparative advantage can be wearing–and cruel. It leaves behind losers in concentrated clumps* (a closed tyre factory, for instance), whereas the more numerous winners (everybody driving cheaper cars) are disparate*. It makes the wealthy very wealthy: in a global market, you will hit a bigger jackpot than in a local one. And capitalism has always been prone to[5)] spectacular* booms and busts.[6)]

11. Above all[7)] politics remains stubbornly local. All that economic integration has not been matched politically. And to the extent

reverse [rivə́:rs]: 거꾸로 되다, 반대가 되다
franchise [frǽntʃaiz]: 가맹점 영업권, 독점 사업권
surge [sə:rdʒ]: 큰 파도, 격동; 밀려들다, 휩싸다
clump [klʌmp]: 무리; 쿵(하는 발자국 소리), (발로) 쿵쾅거리다
disparate [díspərit]: (본질적으로) 다른, 이질적인 부분들로 이뤄진
spectacular [spektǽkjələ:r]: 장관을 이루는, 화려한

1) put another way: 다른 말로 바꾸어서
2) catch up with: 진도를 따라잡다
3) unreservedly: 서슴없이, 단호하게
4) face up to: 직면하다
5) be prone to ~: ~하기 쉽다, ~의 경향이 있다
6) boom and bust: 번영과 불황
7) above all: 다른 무엇보다도 특히, 우선 첫째로

that[1] there is a global guarantor* of the current system, it is America, a country which as globalization works will continue to lose relative power. Thanks to its generosity in exporting the secrets of success, it now has China closer to its shoulder and other emerging giants are catching up. Public support for protectionism* has surged* in the United States.

12. In the affairs of man, wounded pride and xenophobia* often trump* economic reason. Why else would Russia terrorise its gas customers? Or Britons demonise the EU? In a rational world China would not stir up Japanophobia[2] and rich Saudis would not help Islamic extremists abroad. Many businesspeople, too busy on their BlackBerrys to worry about nationalism or fundamentalism, might ponder* Keynes's description of a prosperous Londoner before August 1914: sipping his morning tea in bed, ordering goods from around the world over the telephone, regarding that age of globalization as "normal, certain, and permanent, except in the direction of further improvement" and dismissing* "the politics of militarism" and "racial and cultural rivalries" as mere "amusements in his daily newspaper".

Be prepared, be very prepared

13. Recognising the political shortcomings* of globalization should

guarantor [gæ̀rəntɔ́:r]: 보증인
protectionism [prətékʃənzəm]: (무역) 보호주의
surge [sə:rdʒ]: (재빨리) 밀려들다, (강한 감정이) 휩싸다, (강한 감정이) 치밀어 오름
xenophobia [zènəfóubiə] : 외국인 혐오(증)
trump [trʌmp]: 으뜸패를 내놓다 [치다]; 마지막 수단을 쓰다
ponder [pɑ́ndər]: 숙고하다, 곰곰이 생각하다
dismiss [dismís]: 묵살하다, 떨쳐 버리다
shortcomingʃɔ́:rtkʌ̀miŋ]: 결점, 모자라는 점

1) to the extent that ~: ~의 한도까지, ~만큼
2) Japanophobia: Japan + xenophobia 합성어

redouble Western liberals' determination to defend it: to close the gap in the right way. That involves a myriad of[1] things, from promoting human rights to designing better jobs policies. But it also requires defending the enormous benefits that capitalism has brought the world since 1989 more forcefully than the West's leaders have done thus far. And above all perhaps, taking nothing for granted.

1) a myriad of: 무수한

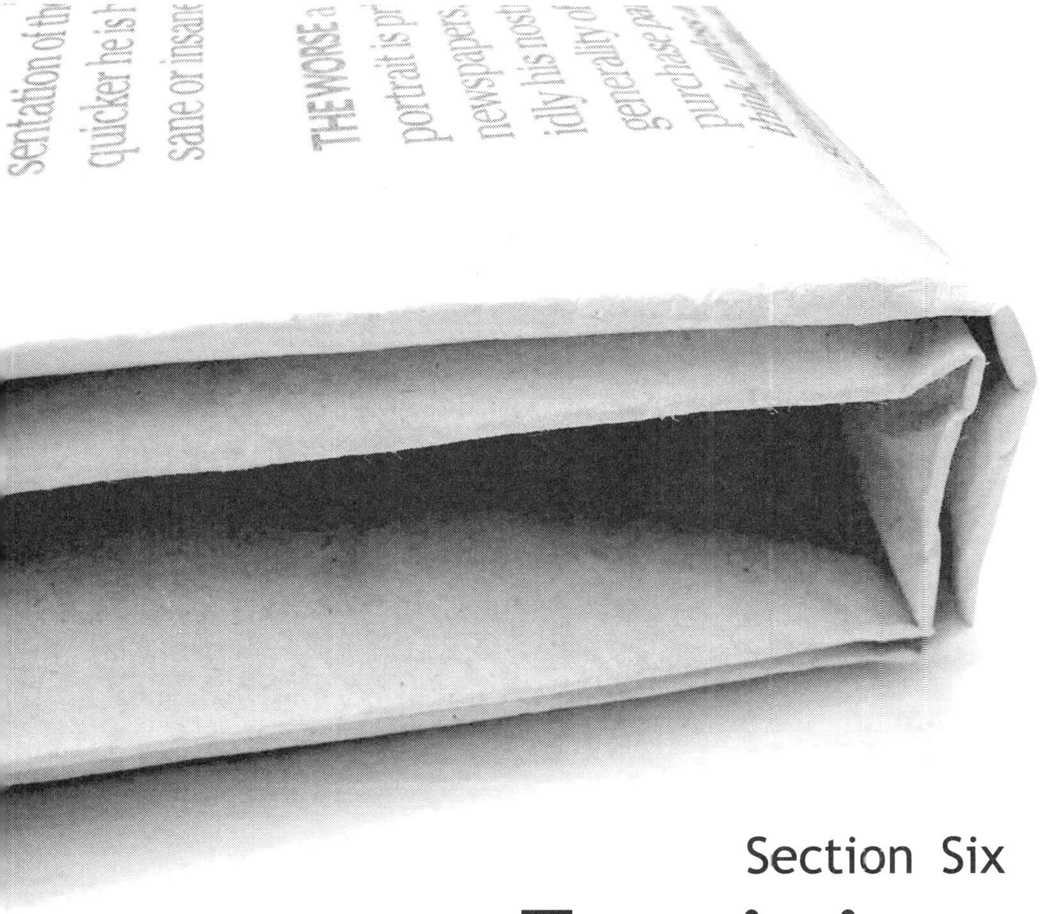

Section Six

Feminism

1. Womenomics

Feminist management theorists are flirting* with some dangerous arguments

1. The late Paul Samuelson[1] once quipped* that "women are just men with less money". As a father of six, he might have added something about women's role in the reproduction of the species.[2] But his aphorism* is about as good a one-sentence summary of classical feminism as you can get.[3]

2. The first generations of successful women insisted on being judged by the same standards as men. They had nothing but contempt for the notion of special treatment for "the sisters", and instead insisted on getting ahead by dint of[4] working harder and thinking smarter. Margaret Thatcher made no secret of her contempt for the wimpish* men around her. (There is a joke about her going out to dinner with her cabinet.[5] "Steak or fish?" asks the waiter. "Steak, of course," she replies. "And for the vegetables?" "They'll have steaks as well.") During America's most recent presidential election Hillary Clinton taunted* Barack

flirt [flə́ːrt]: 희롱하다, 시시덕거리다
quip [kwip]: 재담, 재담을 하다
aphorism [ǽfərìzəm]: 경구
wimpish [wíkmpiʃ]: 나약한, 겁쟁이의

1) 노벨 경제학상을 수상한 미국 경제학자
2) if 절이 생략된 가정의 의미
3) about (almost) as good ~ as — : 거의 —만큼 좋은 ~이다
4) by dint of ~ : ~에 의해서 (by means of)
5) cabinet: (정부의) 내각

Obama with an advertisement that implied that he, unlike she, was not up to[1] the challenge of answering the red phone[2] at 3 am.

3. Many pioneering businesswomen pride themselves on their toughness.[3] Dong Mingzhu, the boss of Gree Electric Appliances, an air-conditioning giant, says flatly, "I never miss. I never admit mistakes and I am always correct." In the past three years her company has boosted* shareholder* returns by nearly 500%.

4. But some of today's most influential feminists contend that women will never fulfil their potential* if they play by men's rules. According to Avivah Wittenberg-Cox and Alison Maitland, two of the most prominent* exponents* of this position, it is not enough to smash the glass ceiling. You need to audit* the entire building for "gender asbestos"—in other words, root out[4] the inherent* sexism built into corporate structures and processes.

5. The new feminism contends that women are wired differently from men, and not just in trivial ways. They are less aggressive and more consensus-seeking, less competitive and more collaborative*, less power-obsessed and more group-oriented. Judy Rosener, of the University of California, Irvine, argues that women excel* at

taunted [tɔːnt]: 비웃다, 조롱하다
boost [buːst]: 신장시키다, 북돋우다
shareholder [ʃέərhòuldəːr]: 주주
potential [pouténʃəl]: 가능성(이 있는), 잠재적인
prominent [prámənənt]: 유명한, 눈에 잘 띄는, 두드러진
exponents [ikspóunənt]: (사상 · 학설 등의) 주창자
audit [ɔ́ːdit]: 회계 감사 (하다)
inherent [inhíərənt]: 내재하는
collaborative [kəlǽbərèitiv]: 공동의, 협동적인
excel [iksél]: 뛰어나다, 탁월하다

1) be up to something: be as good as people expect; ~ 할 만한 자질이 있다
be up to somebody: ~가 할 [결정할]일이다
2) The red phone linked the White House via the National Military Command Center with the Kremlin during the Cold War.
3) pride oneself on ~: be proud of ~, ~을 자랑스러워하다
4) root out: 뿌리째 뽑다

"transformational" and "interactive" management. Peninah Thomson and Jacey Graham, the authors of "A Women's Place is in the Boardroom",[1] assert that women are "better lateral* thinkers than men" and "more idealistic" into the bargain[2]. Feminist texts are suddenly full of references* to tribes of monkeys, with their aggressive males and nurturing* females.

6. What is more,[3] the argument runs, these supposedly womanly qualities are becoming ever more valuable in business. The recent financial crisis proved that the sort of qualities that men pride themselves on, such as risk-taking and bare-knuckle competition,[4] can lead to disaster. Lehman Brothers would never have happened if it had been Lehman Sisters, according to this theory. Even before the financial disaster struck, the new feminists also claim, the best companies had been abandoning "patriarchal*" hierarchies* in favour of "collaboration" and "networking" skills in which women have an inherent advantage.

7. This argument may sound a little like the stuff of gender workshops in righteous universities. But it is gaining followers in powerful places. McKinsey, the most venerable* of management consultancies, has published research arguing that women apply five of the nine "leadership behaviours" that lead to corporate success more frequently than men. Niall FitzGerald, the chairman of Reuters and a former boss of Unilever, is as close as you can get to[5] the heart of the corporate establishment. He proclaims, "Women have different ways of achieving results, and leadership

lateral [lǽt-ərəl]: 옆의, 측면의
reference [réf-ərəns]: 언급, 참고, 참조
nurture [nə́:rtʃə:r]: 양육하다, 육성하다
patriarchal [péitriɑ̀:rkəl]: 가부장제의, 가부장적인 (反 matriarchal)
hierarchy [háiərɑ̀:rki]: (특히 사회나 조직 내의) 계급
venerable [vénərəbəl]: 존경할 만한, 덕망 있는

1) boardroom: 중역(회의)실
2) into(in) the bargain: 게다가, 그 위에
3) what is more: 게다가
4) bare-knuckle competition: 맨주먹으로 하는 경쟁
5) as close as you can get to ~: ~ 로 가장 가까이 가다

qualities that are becoming more important as our organizations become less hierarchical and more loosely organised around matrix* structures." Many companies are abandoning the old-fashioned commitment to treating everybody equally and instead becoming "gender adapted" and "gender bilingual"—in touch with the unique management wisdom of their female employees. A host of[1] consultancies has sprung up to teach firms how to listen to women and exploit* their special abilities.

8. The new feminists are right to be frustrated about the pace of women's progress in business. Britain's Equality and Human Rights Commission calculated that, at the current rate of progress, it will take 60 years for women to gain equal representation on the boards of the FTSE 100.[2] They are also right that old-fashioned feminism took too little account of[3] women's role in raising children. But their arguments about the innate* differences between men and women are sloppy* and counterproductive.

9. People who bang on about innate differences should remember that variation* within subgroups in the population is usually bigger than the variation between subgroups. Even if it can be established that, on average, women have a higher "emotional-intelligence quotient*" than men, that says little about any specific* woman. Judging people as individuals rather than as representatives of groups is both morally right and good for business.

matrix: matrix [méitriks, mǽt-]: 모체, 기반
exploit [éksplɔit]: 이용하다, 착취하다
innate [inéit]: 타고난, 선천적인
sloppy [slάpi]: 엉성한, 대충하는
variation [vɛ̀əriéiʃən]: 변화, 변이
quotient [kwóuʃənt]: (나눗셈에서) 몫
specific [spisífik]: 구체적인, 특정한

1) a host of : 수많은
2) FTSE 100: (풋시100) 런던 증권거래소 에 상장되어 있는 주식 중, 시가총액 순서대로 100개 기업
3) take account of ~ : ~ 을 고려하다, 참작하다

Caring, sharing and engineering

10. Besides, many of the most successful women are to be found in hard-edged[1] companies, rather than the touchy-feely[2] organisations of the new feminist imagination: Areva (nuclear energy), AngloAmerican (mining), Archer Daniels Midland (agribusiness), Dupont (chemicals), Sunoco (oil) and Xerox (technology) all have female bosses. The Cranfield School of Management's Female FTSE100 Index reveals that two of the industries with the best record for promoting women to their boards are banking and transport.

11. Women would be well advised to ignore the siren voices of the new feminism and listen to Ms Dong instead. Despite their frustration, the future looks bright. Women are now out-performing men markedly in school and university. It would be a grave mistake to abandon old-fashioned meritocracy* just at the time when it is turning to women's advantage.

meritocracy [mèritάkrəsi]: 능력주의 사회; 엘리트 계층

1) hard-edged: 철저하게 현실에 입각한, 냉철한
2) touch-feely: expressing emotions such as love and affection openly

2. We did it!

The rich world's quiet revolution: women are gradually taking over[1] the workplace

1. At a time when the world is short of causes for celebration, here is a candidate: within the next few months women will cross the 50% threshold* and become the majority of the American workforce. Women already make up[2] the majority of university graduates in the OECD countries[3] and the majority of professional workers in several rich countries, including the United States. Women run many of the world's great companies, from PepsiCo in America to Areva in France.

2. Women's economic empowerment* is arguably the biggest social change of our times. Just a generation ago, women were largely confined to repetitive, menial* jobs. They were routinely* subjected to[4] casual sexism and were expected to abandon their careers when they married and had children. Today they are running some of the organizations that once treated them as second-class citizens. Millions of women have been given more control over their own lives. And millions of brains have been put to more productive use. Societies that try to resist this trend — most notably* the Arab countries, but also Japan and some

threshold [əréʃhould]: 문지방, 한계점 / empower [empáuər]: 권력 [권한]을 주다
menial [mí:niəl]: 하찮은, 천한 / routine [ru:tí:n]: 판에 박힌 (일상)
notably [nóutəbli]: 특히, 현저히

1) take over: 양도받다, 점거하다
2) make up: 구성하다
3) OECD: Organization for Economic Co-operation and Development
4) be subjected to ~: ~에 종속되다

southern European countries—will pay a heavy price in the form of wasted talent and frustrated citizens.

3. This revolution has been achieved with only a modicum* of friction*. Men have, by and large,[1] welcomed women's invasion of the workplace. Yet even the most positive changes can be incomplete or unsatisfactory. This particular advance comes with two stings*. The first is that women are still under-represented at the top of companies. Only 2% of the bosses of America's largest companies and 5% of their peers* in Britain are women. They are also paid significantly less than men on average. The second is that juggling* work and child-rearing is difficult. Middle-class couples routinely complain that they have too little time for their children. But the biggest losers are poor children—particularly in places like America and Britain that have combined high levels of female participation in the labour force with a reluctance* to spend public money on child care.

Dealing with the juggle

4. These two problems are closely related. Many women feel they have to choose between their children and their careers. Women who prosper* in high-pressure companies during their 20s drop out in dramatic numbers in their 30s and then find it almost impossible to regain their earlier momentum*. Less-skilled women

modicum [mάdikəm]: 소량, 근소
friction [fríkʃ-ən]: 마찰, 저항
sting [stiŋ]: 찌르기, 찌르다, 침, 가시
peer [piər]: 또래, 동년배
juggle [dʒʌ́gəl]: (두 가지 이상의 일을 동시에) 곡예 하듯 하다
reluctance [rilʌ́ktəns]: 마지못해 함, 마음 내키지 않음
prosper [prάspər]: 번영, 번성하다
momentum [mouméntəm]: (일의 진행의) 탄력, 가속도

1) by and large: 대체로 (on the whole)

are trapped in poorly paid jobs with hand-to-mouth[1)] child-care arrangements. Motherhood, not sexism, is the issue: in America, childless women earn almost as much as men, but mothers earn significantly less. And those mothers' relative* poverty also disadvantages their children.

5. Demand for female brains is helping to alleviate* some of these problems. Even if some of the new theories about warm-hearted women making inherently superior workers are bunk*, several trends favour the more educated sex, including the "war for talent" and the growing flexibility* of the workplace. Law firms, consultancies and banks are rethinking their "up or out"[2)] promotion systems because they are losing so many able women. More than 90% of companies in Germany and Sweden allow flexible working. And new technology is making it easier to redesign work in all sorts of family-friendly[3)] ways.

6. Women have certainly performed better over the past decade than men. In the European Union women have filled 6m of the 8m new jobs created since 2000. In America three out of four people thrown out of work since the "mancession"[4)] began have been male. And the shift towards women is likely to continue: by 2011 there will 2.6m more female than male university students in America.

relative [rélətiv]: 비교상의, 상대적인
alleviate [əlí:vièit]: 완화하다
bunk [bʌŋk]: 허풍 (nonsense)
flexibility [flèksəbíləti]: 유연성, 다루기 쉬움

1) hand-to-mouth: 그날그날 살아가는, 생활에 여유가 없는
2) up or out: 승진 혹은 퇴출
3) family-friendly: 가족친화적인
4) mancession: male unemployment

The light hand of the state

7. All this argues, mostly, for letting the market do the work. That has not stopped calls for hefty* state intervention of the Scandinavian sort. Norway has used threats of quotas to dramatic effect. Some 40% of the legislators there are women. All the Scandinavian countries provide plenty of state-financed nurseries*. They have the highest levels of female employment in the world and far fewer of the social problems that plague* Britain and America. Surely, comes the argument, there is a way to speed up the revolution—and improve the tough lives of many working women and the children?

8. If that means massive intervention, in the shape of affirmative-action[1] programmes and across-the-board[2] benefits for parents of all sorts, the answer is no. To begin with,[3] promoting people on the basis of their sex is illiberal and unfair, and stigmatizes* its beneficiaries*. And there are practical problems. Lengthy periods of paid maternity leave[4] can put firms off hiring women, which helps explain why most Swedish women work in the public sector and Sweden has a lower proportion of women in management than America does.

9. But there are plenty of cheaper, subtler ways in which governments can make life easier for women. Welfare states were designed when most women stayed at home. They need to change the way they operate. German schools, for instance, close at

hefty [héfti]: 장대한; 크고 무거운
nursery [nə́:rs-əri]: 아기방, 유치원
plague [pleig]: 전염병, 괴롭히다
stigmatize [stígmətàiz]: 오명을 씌우다, 낙인찍다
beneficiary [bènəfíʃièri]: 수혜자, (유산) 수령인

1) affirmative action: 차별 철폐 조처 (소수 민족과 여성의 교육 기회와 고용에 있어서)
2) across-the-board: 모든를 포함하는, 일괄적인
3) to begin with: 우선, 먼저
4) maternity leave: 출산 휴가

midday. American schools shut down for two months in the summer. These things can be changed without huge cost. Some popular American charter schools[1] now offer longer school days and shorter summer holidays. And, without going to Scandinavian lengths,[2] America could invest more in its children: it spends a lower share of its GDP on public child-care than almost any other rich country, and is the only rich country that refuses to provide mothers with paid maternity leave. Barack Obama needs to measure up to[3] his campaign rhetoric* about "real family values".

10. Still, these nagging problems should not overshadow the dramatic progress that women have made in recent decades. During the second world war, when America's menfolk were off at the front, the government had to summon up the image of Rosie the Riveter, with her flexed muscle and "We Can Do It" slogan, to encourage women into the workforce. Today women are marching into the workplace in ever larger numbers and taking a sledgehammer to the remaining glass ceilings.

rhetoric [rétərik]: 미사여구, 수사법

1) charter school: 독자 운영되는 공립 학교
2) without ~ lengths: ~ 정도까지 안가더라도
3) measure up to ~: ~에 달하다. ~에 일치 [부합]하다

Section Seven

Great Speeches

1. Barack Obama : Inaugural Address

"Time has come to reaffirm our enduring spirit"

Jan. 20, 2009
WASHINGTON

1. My fellow citizens,

2. I stand here today humbled by the task before us, grateful for the trust you have bestowed*, mindful of[1] the sacrifices borne by our ancestors. I thank President Bush for his service to our nation, as well as the generosity* and cooperation he has shown throughout this transition*.

3. Forty-four Americans have now taken the presidential oath. The words have been spoken during rising tides of prosperity* and the still waters of peace. Yet, every so often the oath is taken amidst gathering clouds and raging storms. At these moments, America has carried on not simply because of the skill or vision of those in high office,[2] but because we the People have remained faithful to the ideals of our forbearers, and true to our founding documents.[3]

4. So it has been. So it must be with this generation of Americans. That we are in the midst of crisis is now well understood.

bestow [bistóu]: 수여하다, 부여하다
generosity [dʒènərάsəti]: 너그러움
transition [trænzíʃən]: 과도기, 전환기
prosperity [prαspérəti]: 번영, 번성, 번창

1) mindful of~: ~을 염두에 두고, ~을 기리며
2) those in high office: 고위 공직자
3) founding documents: 건국 문서

Our nation is at war, against a far-reaching[1)] network of violence and hatred. Our economy is badly weakened, a consequence of **greed*** and irresponsibility on the part of some, but also our **collective*** failure to make hard choices and prepare the nation for a new age. Homes have been lost; jobs shed; businesses shuttered. Our health care is too costly; our schools fail too many; and each day brings further evidence that the ways we use energy strengthen our **adversaries*** and threaten our planet.

5. These are the indicators of crisis, subject to[2)] data and **statistics***. Less measurable but no less profound[3)] is a sapping of confidence[4)] across our land[5)] — a **nagging*** fear that America's decline is inevitable, and that the next generation must lower its sights.

6. Today I say to you that the challenges we face are real. They are serious and they are many. They will not be met easily or in a short span of time. But know this, America — they will be met.[6)]

7. On this day, we gather because we have chosen hope over fear, unity of purpose over conflict and **discord***.

8. On this day, we come to **proclaim*** an end to the petty **grievances*** and false promises, the **recriminations*** and worn out[7)] dogmas, that for far too long have **strangled*** our politics.

greed [gri:d]: 탐욕
collective [kəléktiv]: 집단의, 단체의
adversary [ǽdzvərsèri]: 상대방, 적수
statistics [stətístiks]: 통계
nagging [nǽgiŋ]: 계속되는, 없어지지 않는
discord [dískɔ:rd]: 불화, 다툼
proclaim [proukléim]: 선언하다, 선포하다
grievance [grí:vəns]: 불만, 고충

1) far-reaching: 멀리 뻗은
2) subject to: 지배를 받는, 의존하는
3) less m~able but no less p~: 측정하기 어려우나 못지 않게, 심각한
4) sap: 수액, —에서 활력을 없애다, 약화시키다
sapping of confidence: 자신감이 빠져나감
5) CVS 의 도치된 문장구조
6) meet; 대처하다, 맞서다
7) worn out: 낡은

9. We remain a young nation, but in the words of Scripture, the time has come to set aside[1)] childish things. The time has come to reaffirm* our enduring spirit; to choose our better history; to carry forward that precious gift, that noble idea, passed on from generation to generation: the God-given promise that all are equal, all are free, and all deserve a chance to pursue their full measure of happiness.

10. In reaffirming the greatness of our nation, we understand that greatness is never a given.[2)] It must be earned. Our journey has never been one of short-cuts or settling for less.[3)] It has not been the path for the faint-hearted — for those who prefer leisure over work, or seek only the pleasures of riches and fame. Rather, it has been the risk-takers, the doers, the makers of things — some celebrated[4)] but more often men and women obscure in their labor, who have carried us up the long, rugged path towards prosperity and freedom.

11. For us, they packed up their few worldly possessions and traveled across oceans in search of a new life.

12. For us, they toiled in sweatshops* and settled the West; endured the lash of the whip and plowed the hard earth.

13. For us, they fought and died, in places like Concord and Gettysburg; Normandy and Khe Sahn.[5)]

14. Time and again these men and women struggled and sacrificed and worked till their hands were raw so that we might

recriminate [rikrímənèit]: 비난, 맞대응하다
strangle [strǽŋgəl]: 목을 조르다, 질식시키다
reaffirm [rì:əfə́:rm]: 재차 확인하다, 확언하다
sweatshop [swétʃɑ̀p]: 노동력 착취의 현장

1) set aside: 버리다, 거절하다
2) given: 그냥 주어진 것
3) settle for less: 덜한(작은) 것에 안주하다
4) celebrated: p.p. 로 사용
5) 각기 미국이 치른 4개의 중요한 전쟁을 대표하는 격전지경
Khe Sahn 은 Bruce Springsteen 의 "Born in the U. S. A." 가사에도 등장하는 월남전의 대표격전지임

live a better life. They saw America as bigger than the sum of our individual ambitions; greater than all the differences of birth or wealth or faction*.

15. This is the journey we continue today. We remain the most prosperous, powerful nation on Earth. Our workers are no less[1] productive than when this crisis began. Our minds are no less inventive, our goods and services no less needed than they were last week or last month or last year. Our capacity remains undiminished*. But our time of standing pat,[2] of protecting narrow interests and putting off unpleasant decisions — that time has surely passed. Starting today, we must pick ourselves up,[3] dust ourselves off, and begin again the work of remaking America.

16. For everywhere we look, there is work to be done. The state of the economy calls for action, bold and swift, and we will act — not only to create new jobs, but to lay a new foundation for growth. We will build the roads and bridges, the electric grids[4] and digital lines[5] that feed our commerce and bind us together. We will restore science to its rightful place, and wield technology's wonders to raise health care's quality and lower its cost. We will harness* the sun and the winds and the soil to fuel our cars and run our factories. And we will transform our schools and colleges and universities to meet the demands[6] of a new age. All this we can do. All this we will do.

17. Now, there are some who question the scale of our ambitions — who suggest that our system cannot tolerate too many big plans. Their memories are short. For they have forgotten what this

faction [fǽkʃən]: 파벌, 당파 / diminish [dimíniʃ]: 줄이다, 감소시키다, 감소하다
harness [hɑ́:rnis]: (동력원 등으로) 이용하다, 활용하다

1) no less ~ than: 덜 ~ 한건 아니다, 마찬가지로 ~ 하다
2) stand pat: (의견을) 굽히지 않다, 고집부리다
3) pick oneself up: 심기충전하다, 스스로를 추스리다
4) electric grids: 전력망
5) digital lines: 통신망
6) meet the demands: 요구에 응하다

country has already done; what free men and women can achieve when imagination is joined to common purpose, and necessity[1] to courage.

18. What the cynics fail to understand is that the ground has shifted beneath them — that the **stale*** political arguments that have consumed us for so long no longer apply. The question we ask today is not whether our government is too big or too small, but whether it works — whether it helps families find jobs at a decent wage, care they can afford, a retirement that is dignified. Where the answer is yes, we intend to move forward. Where the answer is no, programs will end. And those of us who manage the public's dollars will be held to account[2] — to spend wisely, reform bad habits, and do our business in the light of day[3] — because only then can we restore the vital trust between a people and their government.

19. Nor is the question before us whether the market is a force for good or ill. Its power to generate wealth and expand freedom is unmatched,[4] but this crisis has reminded us that without a watchful eye, the market can spin out of control[5] — and that a nation cannot prosper long when it favors only the prosperous. The success of our economy has always depended not just on the size of our Gross Domestic Product, but on the reach[6] of our prosperity; on the ability to extend opportunity to every willing heart — not out of charity, but because it is the surest route to our common good.

20. As for our common defense, we reject as false the choice between our safety and our ideals. Our Founding Fathers,[7] faced

stale [steil]: 신선미가 없는, 진부한, 김이 빠진

1) necessity (is joined 생략)
2) hold ~ to account: ~ 에게 책임을 지우다
3) in the light of day: 투명하게
4) unmatched: 필적할 수 없는, 비길 데 없는
5) spin out of control: 통제권을 벗어나다
6) reach: (행동 · 능력 · 권력 따위의) 미치는 [유효]범위
7) founding fathers: 건국의 아버지들

with perils* we can scarcely imagine, drafted a charter to assure* the rule of law and the rights of man, a charter expanded by the blood of generations. Those ideals still light the world, and we will not give them up for expedience's* sake. And so to all other peoples and governments who are watching today, from the grandest capitals to the small village where my father was born: know that America is a friend of each nation and every man, woman, and child who seeks a future of peace and dignity, and we are ready to lead once more.

21. Recall that earlier generations faced down[1] fascism and communism not just with missiles and tanks, but with sturdy* alliances* and enduring convictions.[2] They understood that our power alone cannot protect us, nor does it entitle* us to do as we please. Instead, they knew that our power grows through its prudent* use; our security emanates* from the justness of our cause, the force of our example, the tempering* qualities of humility* and restraint*.

22. We are the keepers of this legacy*. Guided by[3] these principles once more, we can meet those new threats that demand even greater effort — even greater cooperation and understanding between nations. We will begin to responsibly leave Iraq to its

peril [pérəl]: 위험, 위태
assure [əʃúər]: 보장하다, 확약하다
expedience [ikspí:diəns]: 편의주의
sturdy [stə́:rdi]: 튼튼한, 견고한
alliance [əláiəns]: 동맹, 연합
entitle [entáitl]: 자격을 주다, 권한을 주다
prudent [prú:dənt]: 신중한
emanate [émənèit]: 발산하다, (생각·명령 등이) 나오다
temper [témpə:r]: (칼 따위를) 담금질하다; (사람을) 단련시키다, 유연해지다
humility [hju:míləti]: 겸손
restraint [ristréint]: 자제, 규제 / legacy [légəsi]: 유산

1) face down: 진압, 제압하다
2) enduring conviction: 지속적인 신념, 확신
3) (As we are) guided by

people, and forge* a hard-earned peace in Afghanistan. With old friends and former foes, we will work tirelessly to lessen the nuclear threat, and roll back[1] the specter of a warming planet. We will not apologize* for our way of life, nor will we waver* in its defense, and for those who seek to advance their aims by inducing terror and slaughtering* innocents, we say to you now that our spirit is stronger and cannot be broken; you cannot outlast* us, and we will defeat you.

23. For we know that our patchwork heritage[2] is a strength, not a weakness. We are a nation of Christians and Muslims, Jews and Hindus — and non-believers. We are shaped by every language and culture, drawn from every end of this Earth; and because we have tasted the bitter swill of civil war and segregation*, and emerged* from that dark chapter stronger and more united, we cannot help but[3] believe that the old hatreds shall someday pass; that the lines of tribe shall soon dissolve*; that as the world grows smaller, our common humanity shall reveal itself; and that America must play its role in ushering* in a new era of peace.

24. To the Muslim world, we seek a new way forward, based on mutual* interest and mutual respect. To those leaders around the globe who seek to sow conflict, or blame their society's ills on the West — know that your people will judge you on what you can build, not what you destroy. To those who cling to

forge [fɔ:rdʒ]: 1.위조하다; 날조하다 2. (합의·친교 등을) 맺다 3. (쇠를) 벼리다
apologize [əpɑ́lədʒàiz]: 사과하다
waver [wéivə:r]: 약하다, 약해지다,
slaughter [slɔ́:tə:r]: 대량 학살
outlast [àutlǽst]: …보다 더 오래 가다, 계속 가다
segregation [sègrigéiʃ-ən]: 분리, 차별(정책)
emerge [imə́:rdʒ]: 나오다, 모습을 드러내다
dissolve [dizɑ́lv]: 사라지다, 용해되다
usher [ʌ́ʃər]: 안내하다, 선도하다

1) roll back: 뒤로 몰아내다, 쫓아내다
2) patchwork heritage: 다양한 문화유산
3) cannot help but ~: ~ 하지 않을 수 없다

power through corruption and deceit* and the silencing of dissent*, know that you are on the wrong side of history; but that we will extend a hand if you are willing to unclench your fist.

25. To the people of poor nations, we pledge* to work alongside you to make your farms flourish* and let clean waters flow; to nourish starved bodies and feed hungry minds. And to those nations like ours that enjoy relative plenty,[1] we say we can no longer afford indifference to suffering outside our borders; nor can we consume the world's resources without regard to[2] effect. For the world has changed, and we must change with it.

26. As we consider the road that unfolds before us, we remember with humble gratitude* those brave Americans who, at this very hour, patrol far-off deserts and distant mountains. They have something to tell us, just as the fallen heroes who lie in Arlington[3] whisper through the ages. We honor them not only because they are guardians of our liberty, because they embody the spirit of service; a willingness to find meaning in something greater than themselves. And yet, at this moment — a moment that will define a generation — it is precisely this spirit that must inhabit us all.

27. For as much as government can do and must do, it is ultimately* the faith and determination of the American people upon which this nation relies.[4] It is the kindness to take in a stranger

mutual [mjú:tʃuəl]: 상호간의, 서로의
deceit [disí:t]: 속임수, 사기, 기만
dissent [disént]: 불찬성, 이의(를 말하다)
pledge [pledʒ]: 약속하다, 맹세하다
flourish [flə́:riʃ, flʌ́riʃ]: 번창하다
gratitude [grǽtətjù:d]: 감사, 사의
ultimately [ʌ́ltəmitli]:최후로, 결국, 궁극적으로

1) relative plenty: 비교적 풍요로움
2) without regard to ~: ~에 관계없이, ~을 고려하지 않고
3) Arlington National Cemetery
4) rely on (upon) ~: ~에 의존하다

when the levees* break, the selflessness of workers who would rather cut their hours than see a friend lose their job which sees us through our darkest hours.[1] It is the firefighter's courage to storm[2] a stairway filled with smoke, but also a parent's willingness to nurture* a child, that finally decides our fate.[3]

28. Our challenges may be new. The instruments with which we meet them may be new. But those values upon which our success depends — honesty and hard work, courage and fair play, tolerance and curiosity, loyalty and patriotism — these things are old. These things are true. They have been the quiet force of progress throughout our history. What is demanded then is a return to these truths. What is required of us now is a new era of responsibility — a recognition, on the part of every American, that we have duties to ourselves, our nation, and the world, duties that we do not grudgingly* accept but rather seize gladly, firm in the knowledge that there is nothing so satisfying to the spirit, so defining of our character, than giving our all to a difficult task.

29. This is the price and the promise of citizenship.

30. This is the source of our confidence— the knowledge that God calls on us to shape an uncertain destiny.

31. This is the meaning of our liberty and our creed* — why men and women and children of every race and every faith can join in celebration across this magnificent mall,[4] and why a man whose father less than sixty years ago might not have been served at a local restaurant can now stand before you to take a most sacred oath.

levee [lévi]: (강가의) 제방 / nurture [nə́:rtʃə:r]: 양육 (하다)
grudgingly [grʌ́dʒiŋli]: 마지못하게, 달갑지 않게
creed [kri:d]: 교의, 신조

1) It is ~ which ...: ... 는 바로 ~ 이다 (~ 강조)
2) storm: 돌격하다, 돌진하다
3) It is ~ that ...: ... 은 바로 ~ 이다 (~ 강조)
4) 취임연설이 행해지고 있는 Capitol Hall 앞의 광장

32. So let us mark this day with remembrance, of who we are and how far we have traveled. In the year of America's birth, in the coldest of months, a small band of patriots huddled1) by dying campfires on the shores of an icy river. The capital was abandoned. The enemy was advancing. The snow was stained with blood. At a moment when the outcome of our revolution was most in doubt, the father of our nation ordered these words be read to the people:

33. "Let it be told to the future world ... that in the depth of winter, when nothing but hope and virtue could survive ... that the city and the country, alarmed at one common danger, came forth to meet [it]."

34. America. In the face of our common dangers, in this winter of our hardship*, let us remember these timeless words. With hope and virtue, let us brave2) once more the icy currents, and endure what storms may come. Let it be said by our children's children that when we were tested we refused to let this journey end, that we did not turn back nor did we falter*; and with eyes fixed on the horizon and God's grace upon us, we carried forth that great gift of freedom and delivered it safely to future generations.

35. Thank you. God bless you. And God bless the United States of America.

hardship [hάːrdʃip]: 고난, 고초
falter [fɔ́ːltər]: 발에 걸려 넘어지다(stumble), 머뭇거리다(hesitate)

1) huddled: 몸을 움츠리고 모여서
2) brave: 용감히 맞서다

2. Barack Obama: Nobel Peace Prize Acceptance Speech

Dec. 12, 2009.
Oslo, Norway

1. Your Majesties, Your Royal Highnesses, Distinguished Members of the Norwegian Nobel Committee, citizens of America, and citizens of the world:

2. I receive this honor with deep gratitude* and great humility*. It is an award that speaks to[1] our highest aspirations*— that for all the cruelty and hardship* of our world, we are not mere prisoners of fate. Our actions matter,[2] and can bend history in the direction of justice.

3. And yet I would be remiss* if I did not acknowledge the considerable controversy* that your generous decision has generated*. In part, this is because I am at the beginning, and not the end, of my labors on the world stage. Compared to some of the giants of history who have received this prize — Schweitzer and King;

gratitude [grǽtətjùːd]: 고마움, 감사
humility [hjuːmíləti]: 겸손, 겸허
aspiration [æ̀spəréiʃən]: 열망, 염원
hardship [háːrdʃip]: 어려움, 곤란
remiss [rimís]: 태만한, 부주의한
controversy [kɑ́ntrəvə̀ːrsi]: 논란, 논쟁
generate [dʒénərèit]: 발생시키다, 만들어 내다

1) speak to ~: ~에 호소하다
speak to the heart: 마음에 호소하다, 마음을 움직이다
2) matter: are important

Marshall and Mandela — my accomplishments are slight*. And then there are the men and women around the world who have been jailed and beaten in the pursuit of justice; those who toil in humanitarian organizations to relieve* suffering; the unrecognized millions whose quiet acts of courage and compassion* inspire even the most hardened of cynics*. I cannot argue with those who find these men and women — some known, some obscure to all but those they help — to be far more deserving of this honor than I.

4. But perhaps the most profound issue surrounding my receipt of this prize is the fact that I am the Commander-in-Chief[1] of a nation in the midst of two wars. One of these wars is winding down.[2] The other is a conflict that America did not seek; one in which we are joined by 43 other countries — including Norway — in an effort to defend ourselves and all nations from further attacks.

5. Still, we are at war, and I am responsible for the deployment* of thousands of young Americans to battle in a distant land. Some will kill. Some will be killed. And so I come here with an acute* sense of the cost of armed conflict[3] — filled with difficult questions about the relationship between war and peace, and our effort to replace one with the other.[4]

6. These questions are not new. War, in one form or another, appeared with the first man. At the dawn of history, its morality was not questioned; it was simply a fact, like drought or disease

slight [slait]: 약간의, 적은 (=inconsiderable): 대수롭지 않은, 하찮은(=trivial)
relieve [rilíːv]: 완화하다, 줄이다
compassion [kəmpǽʃən]: 연민, 동정심
cynic [sínik]: 냉소가, 부정적인 사람들
deploy [diplɔ́i]: (군대 · 무기를) 배치하다
acute [əkjúːt]: 격심한, 극심한

1) commander-in-chief: 총사령관
2) wind down: 느슨해지다, (전쟁 등)의 긴장이 완화되다
3) the cost of armed conflict: 무력분쟁의 대가
4) one=war; the other=peace

— the manner in which tribes and then civilizations sought power and settled their differences.

7. Over time,1) as codes of law sought to control violence within groups, so did philosophers, clerics and statesmen seek to regulate* the destructive power of war. The concept of a "just war" emerged*, suggesting that war is justified only when it meets2) certain preconditions: if it is waged as a last resort* or in self-defense; if the forces used3) is proportional*; and if, whenever possible, civilians are spared from violence.

8. For most of history, this concept of just war was rarely observed. The capacity of human beings to think up new ways to kill one another proved inexhaustible*, as did our capacity to exempt from mercy4) those who look different or pray to a different God. Wars between armies gave way to5) wars between nations — total wars6) in which the distinction between combatant and civilian became blurred*. In the span of 30 years, such carnage* would twice engulf* this continent.7) And while it is hard to conceive of a cause more just than the defeat of the Third Reich8)

drought [draut]: 가뭄
regulate [régjəlèit]: 규제 [통제/단속]하다
emerge [imə́:rdʒ]: 나오다, 모습을 드러내다
resort [rizɔ́:rt]: 휴양지; 수단, 방책
proportional [prəpɔ́:rʃənəl]: (~에) 비례하는
inexhaustible [inigzɔ́:stəbəl]: 고갈될 줄 모르는, 무궁무진한
blur [blə:r]: 흐릿해지다; 흐릿하게 만들다 (-rr-)
carnage [kɑ́:rnidʒ]: 대학살
engulf [engʌ́lf]: 완전히 에워싸다, 휩싸다

1) over time: 시간이 흐르면서
2) meet: satisfy
3) the forces used: 사용된 무력
4) exempt from ~ : ~로부터 면제하다. 제외하다
exempt from mercy: 가혹하게 대하다
5) give way to: 양보하다, 자리를 내어주다
6) total war: 전면전
7) World War I & II
8) the Third Reich: 제3제국 (1933~1945년 사이, 히틀러 치하의 독일)

and the Axis powers,[1] World War II was a conflict in which the total number of civilians who died **exceeded*** the number of soldiers who **perished***.

9. In the wake of[2] such destruction, and with the **advent*** of the nuclear age, it became clear to victor and vanquished[3] alike that the world needed institutions to prevent another World War. And so, a quarter century after the United States Senate rejected the League of Nations — an idea for which Woodrow Wilson received this Prize — America led the world in constructing an architecture to keep the peace: a Marshall Plan and a United Nations, mechanisms to govern the waging of war, **treaties*** to protect human rights, prevent **genocide*** and restrict the most dangerous weapons.

10. In many ways, these efforts succeeded. Yes, terrible wars have been fought, and **atrocities*** committed. But there has been no Third World War. The Cold War ended with **jubilant*** crowds **dismantling*** a wall.[4] Commerce has stitched much of the world together. Billions have been lifted from poverty. The ideals of liberty, self-determination, equality and the rule of law have haltingly[5] advanced. We are the heirs of the **fortitude*** and foresight of generations past, and it is a **legacy*** for which my own country is rightfully proud.

exceed [iksí:d]: 넘다, 초과하다
perish [périʃ]: 죽다, 사라지다
advent [ǽdvent]: 도래, 출현
treaty [trí:ti]: 조약
genocide [dʒénəsàid]: 집단 학살, 종족 학살

atrocity [ətrάsəti]: 잔혹 행위
jubilant [dʒú:bələnt]: 승리감에 넘치는, 득의만면한
dismantle [dismǽntl]: 분해하다, 해체하다
fortitude [fɔ́:rtətjù:d]: 불굴의 용기
legacy [légəsi]: 유산, 유물

1) the Axis powers: the coalition headed by Germany, Italy, and Japan that opposed the Allied Powers in World War II
2) in the wake of ~: 의 자국을 좇아서; ~의 결과로서
3) vanquished: 패자
4) the Berlin Wall
5) haltingly: 멈칫거리며, 힘겹게

11. A decade into a new century, this old architecture is buckling* under the weight of new threats. The world may no longer shudder* at the prospect of war between two nuclear superpowers, but proliferation* may increase the risk of catastrophe*. Terrorism has long been a tactic*, but modern technology allows a few small men with outsized rage[1] to murder innocents on a horrific* scale.

12. Moreover, wars between nations have increasingly given way to wars within nations. The resurgence* of ethnic or sectarian* conflicts, the growth of secessionist[2] movements, insurgencies* and failed states[3] have increasingly trapped civilians in unending chaos. In today's wars, many more civilians are killed than soldiers; the seeds of future conflict are sown, economies are wrecked, civil societies torn asunder, refugees amassed and children scarred.

13. I do not bring with me today a definitive* solution to the problems of war. What I do know is that meeting these challenges will require the same vision, hard work and persistence* of those men and women who acted so boldly decades ago. And it will require us to think in new ways about the notions of just war and the imperatives* of a just peace.

buckle [bʌ́kəl]: (죔쇠를) 채우다; (열·압력으로) 굽어지다, 휘다
shudder [ʃʌ́də:r]: 몸을 떨다, 몸서리치다
proliferation [proulífərèiʃən]: 급증, 확산
catastrophe [kətǽstrəfi]: 참사, 재앙
tactic [tǽktik]: 전략, 작전
horrific [hɔ:rífik]: 무서운, 대단한
resurgence [risə́:rrdʒəntəns]: 재기, 부활
sectarian [sektέ-əriən]: 종파의
insurgency [insə́:rdʒənsi]: 모반, 폭동
definitive [difínətiv]: 최종적인, 확정적인
persistence [pə:rsístəns]: 끈질김, 집요함
imperative [impérətiv]: 반드시 해야 하는; 불가피한 것

1) outsized rage: 엄청난 분노
2) secessionist: 분리주의자
3) failed states: 실패한 국가

14. We must begin by acknowledging the hard truth that we will not **eradicate*** violent conflict in our lifetimes. There will be times when nations — acting individually or in concert[1] — will find the use of force not only necessary but morally justified.

15. I make this statement mindful of what Martin Luther King said in this same ceremony years ago: "Violence never brings permanent peace. It solves no social problem: It merely creates new and more complicated ones." As someone who stands here as a direct consequence of Dr. King's life's work, I am living **testimony*** to the moral force of non-violence. I know there is nothing weak, nothing passive, nothing **naive*** in the creed and lives of Gandhi and King.

16. But as a head of state sworn to protect and defend my nation, I cannot be guided by their examples alone. I face the world as it is, and cannot stand idle in the face of threats to the American people. For make no mistake: Evil does exist in the world. A nonviolent movement could not have halted Hitler's armies. Negotiations cannot convince al-Qaida's leaders to lay down their arms. To say that force is sometimes necessary is not a call to cynicism — it is a recognition of history, the imperfections of man and the limits of reason.

17. I raise this point because in many countries there is a deep **ambivalence*** about military action today, no matter the cause.[2] At times, this is joined by a **reflexive*** suspicion of America, the world's sole military superpower.

18. Yet the world must remember that it was not simply international institutions — not just treaties and **declarations*** — that

eradicate [irǽdəkèit]: 근절하다, 뿌리 뽑다
testimony [téstəmòuni]: 증거
naive [nɑːíːv]: 순진해 빠진, 순진한
ambivalence [æmbívələns]: (심리) 양면 가치, 반대 감정 병존
reflexive [rifléksiv]: 반사적인
declaration [dèkləréiʃən]: 선언문, 선언, 공표

1) in concert: 함께
2) no matter the cause (may be): 대의가 무엇이던 간에

brought stability* to a post-World War II world. Whatever mistakes we have made, the plain fact is this: The United States of America has helped underwrite* global security for more than six decades with the blood of our citizens and the strength of our arms. The service and sacrifice of our men and women in uniform has promoted peace and prosperity from Germany to Korea, and enabled democracy to take hold in places like the Balkans. We have borne this burden not because we seek to impose* our will. We have done so out of enlightened self-interest — because we seek a better future for our children and grandchildren, and we believe that their lives will be better if other people's children and grandchildren can live in freedom and prosperity.

19. So yes, the instruments of war do have a role to play[1] in preserving* the peace. And yet this truth must coexist with another — that no matter how justified, war promises human tragedy. The soldier's courage and sacrifice is full of glory, expressing devotion to country, to cause and to comrades in arms. But war itself is never glorious, and we must never trumpet it as such.[2]

20. So part of our challenge is reconciling these two seemingly irreconcilable truths — that war is sometimes necessary, and war is at some level an expression of human folly*. Concretely, we must direct our effort to the task that President Kennedy called for long ago. "Let us focus," he said, "on a more practical, more attainable* peace, based not on a sudden revolution in human

stability [stəbíləti]: 안정, 안정성
underwrite [ʌ̀ndəráit]: (비용 부담에) 동의하다
impose [impóuz]: . 부과하다, 강요 [강제]하다
preserve [prizə́ːrv]: 보전하다, 유지하다
folly [fɑ́li]: 판단력 부족, 어리석음
attainable [ətéin]: 이룰 수 있는

1) play a role: 역할을 하다
2) such: glorious

nature but on a gradual* evolution* in human institutions." What might this evolution look like? What might these practical steps be?

21. To begin with,[1] I believe that all nations — strong and weak alike — must adhere to[2] standards that govern the use of force. I — like any head of state[3] — reserve the right to act unilaterally* if necessary to defend my nation. Nevertheless, I am convinced that adhering to standards strengthens those who do, and isolates — and weakens — those who don't.

22. The world rallied* around America after the 9/11 attacks, and continues to support our efforts in Afghanistan, because of the horror of those senseless attacks and the recognized principle of self-defense. Likewise, the world recognized the need to confront Saddam Hussein when he invaded Kuwait — a consensus* that sent a clear message to all about the cost of aggression*.

23. Furthermore, America cannot insist that others follow the rules of the road if we refuse to follow them ourselves. For when we don't, our action can appear arbitrary*, and undercut* the legitimacy* of future intervention* — no matter how justified.

24. This becomes particularly important when the purpose of military action extends beyond self-defense or the defense of one nation against an aggressor. More and more, we all confront

gradual [grǽdʒuəl]: 점진적인, 서서히 일어나는
evolution [èəlúːʃən]: (생물) 진화
unilateral [jùːnəlǽtərəl]: 일방적인, 단독의
rally [rǽli]: 집결(하다)
consensus [kənsénsəs]: 의견일치, 합의
aggression [əgréʃən]: 공격성
arbitrary [ɑ́ːrbitrèri]: 임의적인, 제멋대로인
undercut [ʌ́ndərkʌ̀t]: (충격·효력 등을) 약화하다, 꺾다
legitimacy [lidʒítəməsi]: 합법성, 정당성
intervention [ìntərvénʃən]: 개입, 조정, 중재

1) to begin with: 우선
2) adhere to~: ~을 고수하다; 지지하다
3) head of state: 국가 수반

difficult questions about how to prevent the slaughter* of civilians by their own government, or to stop a civil war whose violence and suffering can engulf an entire region.

25. I believe that force can be justified on humanitarian grounds, as it was in the Balkans, or in other places that have been scarred by war. Inaction tears at our conscience and can lead to more costly intervention later. That is why all responsible nations must embrace[1] the role that militaries with a clear mandate* can play to keep the peace.

26. America's commitment to global security will never waver*. But in a world in which threats are more diffuse*, and missions more complex, America cannot act alone. This is true in Afghanistan. This is true in failed states like Somalia, where terrorism and piracy* is joined by famine and human suffering. And sadly, it will continue to be true in unstable regions for years to come.

27. The leaders and soldiers of NATO countries — and other friends and allies* — demonstrate this truth through the capacity and courage they have shown in Afghanistan. But in many countries, there is a disconnect between the efforts of those who serve and the ambivalence of the broader public. I understand why war is not popular. But I also know this: The belief that peace is desirable is rarely enough to achieve it. Peace requires responsibility. Peace entails* sacrifice. That is why NATO continues to be indispensable. That is why we must strengthen U.N. and regional peacekeeping, and not leave the

slaughter [slɔ́:tə:r]: (가축의) 도살, 도축
mandate [mǽndeit]: 명령 (하다); 위임, 위임 통치령
waver [wéivə:r]: 약해지다, (불안정하게) 흔들리다
diffuse [difjú:z]: 널리 퍼진, 분산된
piracy [páiərəsi]: 해적 행위, 해적질
ally [ǽlai]: 동맹국 [자], 연합국
entail [entéil]: 수반하다

1) embrace: 수용하다

task to a few countries. That is why we honor those who return home from peacekeeping and training abroad to Oslo and Rome; to Ottawa and Sydney; to Dhaka and Kigali — we honor them not as makers of war, but as wagers of peace.

28. Let me make one final point about the use of force. Even as we make difficult decisions about going to war, we must also think clearly about how we fight it. The Nobel Committee recognized this truth in awarding its first prize for peace to Henry Dunant — the founder of the Red Cross, and a driving force[1] behind the Geneva Conventions.

29. Where force is necessary, we have a moral and **strategic*** interest in binding ourselves to certain rules of conduct. And even as we confront a vicious **adversary*** that abides by[2] no rules, I believe that the United States of America must remain a standard bearer in the conduct of war. That is what makes us different from those whom we fight. That is a source of our strength. That is why I **prohibited*** torture. That is why I ordered the prison at Guantanamo Bay closed. And that is why I have reaffirmed America's commitment to abide by the Geneva Conventions. We lose ourselves when we **compromise*** the very ideals that we fight to defend. And we honor those ideals by **upholding*** them not just when it is easy, but when it is hard.

30. I have spoken to the questions that must weigh on our minds and our hearts as we choose to wage war. But let me turn now to our effort to avoid such tragic choices, and speak of three ways that we can build a just and lasting peace.

strategy [strǽtədʒi]: 전략; 책략
adversary [ǽdvərsèri]: (언쟁 · 전투에서) 상대방, 적수
prohibit [prouhíbit]: 금하다, 금지하다
compromise [kάmprəmàiz]: 타협하다, 절충하다
uphold [ʌdphóuld]: 지지하다, 옹호하다

1) driving force: 추동력
2) abide by ~: ~을 지키다, 따르다

31. First, in dealing with those nations that break rules and laws, I believe that we must develop alternatives* to violence that are tough enough to change behavior — for if we want a lasting peace, then the words of the international community must mean something.[1] Those regimes* that break the rules must be held accountable.[2] Sanctions* must exact a real price.[3] Intransigence* must be met with increased pressure — and such pressure exists only when the world stands together as one.

32. One urgent* example is the effort to prevent the spread of nuclear weapons, and to seek a world without them. In the middle of the last century, nations agreed to be bound by a treaty whose bargain is clear: All will have access to peaceful nuclear power;[4] those without nuclear weapons will forsake them; and those with nuclear weapons will work toward disarmament*. I am committed to upholding this treaty.[5] It is a centerpiece of my foreign policy. And I am working with President Medvedev to reduce America and Russia's nuclear stockpiles.

33. But it is also incumbent upon all of us to insist that nations like Iran and North Korea do not game[6] the system. Those who claim to respect international law cannot avert* their eyes when those laws are flouted*. Those who care for their own security

alternative [ɔːltə́ːrnətiv]: 대안, 대안이 되는
regime [reiʒíːm]: 정권, 체제
sanction [sǽŋkʃən]: 허가, 승인; (국제법 위반국에 대한) 제재
intransigence, -y [intrǽnsəns]: (정치상의) 비타협적인 태도
urgent [ə́ːrdʒənt]: 긴급한, 시급한
disarmament [disɑ́ːrməmənt]: 무장 해제. 군비 철폐
avert [əvə́ːrt]: 방지하다, 피하다
incumbent [inkʌ́mbənt]: 의지하는, 의무로 지워지는; 현직 [재직]의
flout [flaut]: (법 등을 공공연히) 어기다, 무시하다

1) mean something: 위력이 있다
2) accountable: responsible
3) price: 대가
4) have access to ~: ~ 에 접근할 수 있다
5) be committed to ~= commit oneself to ~: ~ 에 전력을 다하다
6) game: 장난치다, 유린하다

cannot ignore the danger of an arms race[1] in the Middle East or East Asia. Those who seek peace cannot stand idly by as nations arm themselves for nuclear war.

34. The same principle applies to those who violate international law by brutalizing their own people. When there is genocide in Darfur, systematic rape in Congo or repression in Burma — there must be consequences. And the closer we stand together, the less likely we will be faced with the choice between armed intervention[2] and complicity* in oppression.[3]

35. This brings me to a second point — the nature of the peace that we seek. For peace is not merely the absence of visible conflict. Only a just peace based upon the inherent* rights and dignity of every individual can truly be lasting.

36. It was this insight that drove drafters of the Universal Declaration of Human Rights after the Second World War. In the wake of devastation*, they recognized that if human rights are not protected, peace is a hollow promise.

37. And yet all too often, these words are ignored. In some countries, the failure to uphold human rights is excused by the false suggestion that these are Western principles, foreign to[4] local cultures or stages of a nation's development. And within America, there has long been a tension between those who describe themselves as realists or idealists — a tension that suggests a stark choice between the narrow pursuit of interests or an endless campaign to impose our values.

38. I reject this choice. I believe that peace is unstable where citizens are denied the right to speak freely or worship as they

complicity [kəmplísəti]: (범행) 공모
inherent [inhíərənt]: 본래의, 타고난
devastation [dèvəstéiʃən]: 대대적인 파괴, 황폐

1) arms race: 군비경쟁
2) armed intervention: 무력 개입
3) the ~er, the less likely —: ~하면 할수록, 덜 —할 것이다
4) foreign to ~: ~에 이질적인

please, choose their own leaders or assemble without fear. Pent up[1] grievances* fester*, and the suppression* of tribal and religious identity can lead to violence. We also know that the opposite is true. Only when Europe became free did it finally find peace. America has never fought a war against a democracy, and our closest friends are governments that protect the rights of their citizens. No matter how callously defined,[2] neither America's interests — nor the world's — are served by the denial of human aspirations.

39. So even as we respect the unique culture and traditions of different countries, America will always be a voice for those aspirations that are universal. We will bear witness to[3] the quiet dignity of reformers like Aung Sang Suu Kyi; to the bravery of Zimbabweans who cast their ballots in the face of beatings; to the hundreds of thousands who have marched silently through the streets of Iran. It is telling[4] that the leaders of these governments fear the aspirations of their own people more than the power of any other nation. And it is the responsibility of all free people and free nations to make clear to these movements that hope and history are on their side.

40. Let me also say this: The promotion of human rights cannot be about exhortation* alone. At times,[5] it must be coupled with painstaking* diplomacy. I know that engagement with repressive regimes lacks the satisfying purity of indignation*. But I also

grievance [gríːvəns]: 불만, 불평
fester [féstər]: 곪다
suppression [səpréʃən]: 진압, 억제
exhortation [ègzɔːrtéiʃən]: 간곡한 권고, 장려
painstaking [péinztèikiŋ]: 공들인, 힘든
indignation [ìndignéiʃən]: 분개, 분함

1) pent up: 갇힌, 억눌린
2) callously (they are 생략) defined
3) bear witness to ~: ~을 증언하다, ~의 증인이 되다
4) telling: 명백한, 뚜렷한
5) at times: 종종, 때때로

know that sanctions without outreach[1] — and condemnation* without discussion — can carry forward a crippling status quo.[2] No repressive regime can move down a new path unless it has the choice of an open door.

41. In light of[3] the Cultural Revolution's horrors, Nixon's meeting with Mao appeared inexcusable — and yet it surely helped set China on a path where millions of its citizens have been lifted from poverty, and connected to open societies. Pope John Paul's engagement with Poland created space not just for the Catholic Church, but for labor leaders like Lech Walesa. Ronald Reagan's efforts on arms control and embrace of perestroika[4] not only improved relations with the Soviet Union, but empowered dissidents* throughout Eastern Europe. There is no simple formula here. But we must try as best[5] we can to balance isolation and engagement, pressure and incentives*, so that human rights and dignity are advanced over time.[6]

42. Third, a just peace includes not only civil and political rights — it must encompass* economic security and opportunity. For true peace is not just freedom from fear, but freedom from want.

43. It is undoubtedly true that development rarely takes root without security; it is also true that security does not exist where human beings do not have access to enough food, or clean water, or the medicine they need to survive. It does not exist where children cannot aspire to a decent education or a

condemnation [kɑ̀ndemnéiʃən]: 비난
dissident [dísədənt]: 반체제 인사
incentive [inséntiv]: 장려책, 유인
encompass [inkʌ́mpəs]: 포함하다, 아우르다

1) without outreach: 손을 내밀어보지도 않고
2) status quo : 현재의 상황, 현상
3) in light of ~: ~의 관점에서 보면, ~에 비추어볼 때
4) perestroika: 구소련에서의 Gorbachev의 개혁 정책
5) as best (as) we can
6) over time: 오랜 시간에 걸쳐

job that supports a family. The absence of hope can rot a society from within.1)

44. And that is why helping farmers feed their own people — or nations educate their children and care for the sick — is not mere charity. It is also why the world must come together to confront climate change. There is little scientific dispute* that if we do nothing, we will face more drought, famine* and mass displacement that will fuel more conflict for decades. For this reason, it is not merely scientists and activists who call for swift and forceful action — it is military leaders in my country and others who understand that our common security hangs in the balance.2)

45. Agreements among nations. Strong institutions. Support for human rights. Investments in development. All of these are vital ingredients* in bringing about3) the evolution that President Kennedy spoke about. And yet, I do not believe that we will have the will, or the staying power,4) to complete this work without something more — and that is the continued expansion of our moral imagination, an insistence that there is something irreducible5) that we all share.

46. As the world grows smaller, you might think it would be easier for human beings to recognize how similar we are, to understand that we all basically want the same things, that we all hope for the chance to live out our lives with some measure of happiness and fulfillment for ourselves and our families.

dispute [dispjú:t]: 논박, 반론(하다)
famine [fǽmin]: 기근
ingredients [ingrí:diənt]: 재료, 구성요소

1) from within: 속에서부터
2) hang in the balance: 극히 불안정한 상태에 있다; 두개의 가능성중 어느 쪽이 될지 모르는 상태에 있다
3) bring about: 가져오다
4) staying power: 인내력
5) something irreducible: 더 이상 줄일 수 없는 그 무엇

47. And yet, given[1] the dizzying pace of globalization, and the cultural leveling[2] of modernity, it should come as no surprise that people fear the loss of what they cherish about their particular identities — their race, their tribe and, perhaps most powerfully, their religion. In some places, this fear has led to conflict. At times, it even feels like we are moving backwards. We see it in the Middle East, as the conflict between Arabs and Jews seems to harden. We see it in nations that are torn asunder by tribal lines.

48. Most dangerously, we see it in the way that religion is used to justify the murder of innocents by those who have distorted and defiled the great religion of Islam, and who attacked my country from Afghanistan. These extremists are not the first to kill in the name of God; the cruelties of the Crusades[3] are amply recorded. But they remind us that no Holy War can ever be a just war. For if you truly believe that you are carrying out divine will, then there is no need for restraint — no need to spare the pregnant mother, or the medic, or even a person of one's own faith. Such a warped* view of religion is not just incompatible* with the concept of peace, but the purpose of faith — for the one rule that lies at the heart of every major religion is that we do unto others as we would have them do unto us.

49. Adhering to this law of love has always been the core struggle of human nature. We are fallible. We make mistakes, and fall victim to[4] the temptations of pride, and power, and sometimes evil. Even those of us with the best intentions will at times fail to right the wrongs before us.

warped [wɔːrp]: (생각이) 비뚤어진, (형태가) 휜
incompatible [inkəmpǽtəbəl]: (행동 · 생각 등이 근본적으로 달라서) 양립할 수 없는

1) given ~: 「전치사적」 ~ 주어지면, ~ 라고 가정하면
Given time, it can be done. (시간만 있으면 될 수 있는 일이다.)
2) cultural leveling: 문화적 평등화
3) Crusades: 십자군
4) fall victim to ~: ~의 희생이 되다

50. But we do not have to think that human nature is perfect for us to still believe that the human condition can be perfected. We do not have to live in an idealized world to still reach for those ideals that will make it a better place. The nonviolence practiced by men like Gandhi and King may not have been practical or possible in every circumstance, but the love that they preached — their faith in human progress — must always be the North Star that guides us on our journey.

51. For if we lose that faith — if we dismiss it as silly or naive, if we divorce it from the decisions that we make on issues of war and peace — then we lose what is best about humanity. We lose our sense of possibility. We lose our moral compass.

52. Like generations have before us,[1] we must reject that future. As Dr. King said at this occasion so many years ago: "I refuse to accept despair as the final response to the ambiguities* of history. I refuse to accept the idea that the 'isness' of man's present nature makes him morally incapable of reaching up for the eternal 'oughtness' that forever confronts him."[2]

53. So let us reach for the world that ought to be — that spark of the divine that still stirs within each of our souls. Somewhere today, in the here and now, a soldier sees he's outgunned[3] but stands firm to keep the peace. Somewhere today, in this world, a young protestor awaits the brutality of her government, but has the courage to march on. Somewhere today, a mother facing punishing poverty still takes the time to teach her child, who believes that a cruel world still has a place for his dreams.

54. Let us live by their example. We can acknowledge that oppression will always be with us, and still strive for justice. We

ambiguity [æ̀mbigjúːəti]: 애매모호함, 불명료함

1) have (rejected 생략) before ...
2) isness (is + ness): 현재 그러함
outghtness (ought + ness): 그러해야 함
3) outgun: 군사력이 더 우세하다, is outgunned: 군사력이 열세하다

can admit the intractability* of deprivation*, and still strive for dignity. We can understand that there will be war, and still strive for peace. We can do that — for that is the story of human progress; that is the hope of all the world; and at this moment of challenge, that must be our work here on Earth.

intractability [intræ̀ktəbíləti]: 고집스러움, 다루기 힘듦
deprivation [dèprəvéiʃən]: 궁핍, 빈곤

3. John F. Kennedy : Inauguration Address

Jan. 20, 1961

1. Vice President Johnson, Mr. Speaker, Mr. Chief Justice, President Eisenhower, Vice President Nixon, President Truman, reverend clergy, fellow citizens:

2. We observe today not a victory of party, but a celebration of freedom — symbolizing an end, as well as a beginning — signifying renewal, as well as change. For I have sworn before you and Almighty God the same solemn oath our forebears prescribed nearly a century and three-quarters ago.

3. The world is very different now. For man holds in his mortal hands the power to abolish all forms of human poverty and all forms of human life. And yet the same revolutionary beliefs for which our forebears fought are still at issue around the globe — the belief that the rights of man come not from the generosity of the state, but from the hand of God.

4. We dare not forget today that we are the heirs of that first revolution. Let the word go forth from this time and place, to friend and foe alike, that the torch has been passed to a new generation of Americans — born in this century, tempered by war, disciplined by a hard and bitter peace, proud of our ancient heritage, and unwilling to witness or permit the slow undoing of those human rights to which this nation has always been committed, and to which we are committed today at home and around the world. Let every nation know, whether it wishes us well or ill, that we shall pay any price, bear any burden, meet any hardship, support any friend, oppose any foe, to assure the survival and the success of liberty.

5. This much we pledge — and more. To those old allies whose cultural and spiritual origins we share, we pledge the loyalty of faithful friends. United there is little we cannot do in a host of cooperative ventures. Divided there is little we can do — for we dare not meet a powerful challenge at odds and split asunder.

6. To those new states whom we welcome to the ranks of the free, we pledge our word that one form of colonial control shall not have passed away merely to be replaced by a far more iron tyranny. We shall not always expect to find them supporting our view. But we shall always hope to find them strongly supporting their own freedom — and to remember that, in the past, those who foolishly sought power by riding the back of the tiger ended up inside.

7. To those people in the huts and villages of half the globe struggling to break the bonds of mass misery, we pledge our best efforts to help them help themselves, for whatever period is required — not because the Communists may be doing it, not because we seek their votes, but because it is right. If a free society cannot help the many who are poor, it cannot save the few who are rich.

8. To our sister republics south of our border, we offer a special pledge: to convert our good words into good deeds, in a new alliance for progress, to assist free men and free governments in casting off the chains of poverty. But this peaceful revolution of hope cannot become the prey of hostile powers. Let all our neighbors know that we shall join with them to oppose aggression or subversion anywhere in the Americas. And let every other power know that this hemisphere intends to remain the master of its own house.

9. To that world assembly of sovereign states, the United Nations, our last best hope in an age where the instruments of war have far outpaced the instruments of peace, we renew our pledge of support — to prevent it from becoming merely a forum for invective, to strengthen its shield of the new and the weak, and to enlarge the area in which its writ may run. Finally, to

those nations who would make themselves our adversary, we offer not a pledge but a request: that both sides begin anew the quest for peace, before the dark powers of destruction unleashed by science engulf all humanity in planned or accidental self-destruction.

10. We dare not tempt them with weakness. For only when our arms are sufficient beyond doubt can we be certain beyond doubt that they will never be employed.

11. But neither can two great and powerful groups of nations take comfort from our present course — both sides overburdened by the cost of modern weapons, both rightly alarmed by the steady spread of the deadly atom, yet both racing to alter that uncertain balance of terror that stays the hand of mankind's final war.

12. So let us begin anew — remembering on both sides that civility is not a sign of weakness, and sincerity is always subject to proof. Let us never negotiate out of fear, but let us never fear to negotiate.

13. Let both sides explore what problems unite us instead of belaboring those problems which divide us. Let both sides, for the first time, formulate serious and precise proposals for the inspection and control of arms, and bring the absolute power to destroy other nations under the absolute control of all nations. Let both sides seek to invoke the wonders of science instead of its terrors. Together let us explore the stars, conquer the deserts, eradicate disease, tap the ocean depths, and encourage the arts and commerce. Let both sides unite to heed, in all corners of the earth, the command of Isaiah — to "undo the heavy burdens, and [to]let the oppressed go free." And, if a beachhead of cooperation may push back the jungle of suspicion, let both sides join in creating a new endeavor — not a new balance of power, but a new world of law — where the strong are just, and the weak secure, and the peace preserved. All this will not be finished in the first one hundred days. Nor will it be finished in the first one thousand days; nor in the life of this

Administration; nor even perhaps in our lifetime on this planet. But let us begin. In your hands, my fellow citizens, more than mine, will rest the final success or failure of our course. Since this country was founded, each generation of Americans has been summoned to give testimony to its national loyalty. The graves of young Americans who answered the call to service surround the globe. Now the trumpet summons us again — not as a call to bear arms, though arms we need — not as a call to battle, though embattled we are — but a call to bear the burden of a long twilight struggle, year in and year out, "rejoicing in hope; patient in tribulation," a struggle against the common enemies of man: tyranny, poverty, disease, and war itself.

John F. Kennedy's Presidential Inauguration Ceremony

1959 in Senate Office

14. Can we forge against these enemies a grand and global alliance, North and South, East and West, that can assure a more fruitful life for all mankind? Will you join in that historic effort? In the long history of the world, only a few generations have been granted the role of defending freedom in its hour of maximum danger. I do not shrink from this responsibility — I welcome it. I do not believe that any of us would exchange places with any other people or any other generation. The energy, the faith, the devotion which we bring to this endeavor will light our country and all who serve it. And the glow from that fire can truly light the world. And so, my fellow Americans, ask not what your country can do for you; ask what you can do for your country. My fellow citizens of the world, ask not what

America will do for you, but what together we can do for the freedom of man.

15. Finally, whether you are citizens of America or citizens of the world, ask of us here the same high standards of strength and sacrifice which we ask of you. With a good conscience our only sure reward, with history the final judge of our deeds, let us go forth to lead the land we love, asking His blessing and His help, but knowing that here on earth God's work must truly be our own.

4. Martin Luther King, Jr. :

"I Have a Dream"

Aug. 28, 1963

1. I am happy to join with you today in what will go down in history as the greatest demonstration for freedom in the history of our nation.

2. Five score years ago, a great American, in whose symbolic shadow we stand today, signed the Emancipation Proclamation. This momentous decree came as a great beacon light of hope to millions of Negro slaves, who had been seared in the flames of withering injustice. It came as a joyous daybreak to end the long night of their captivity.

3. But one hundred years later, the Negro still is not free. One hundred years later, the life of the Negro is still sadly crippled by the manacles of segregation and the chains of discrimination. One hundred years later, the Negro lives on a lonely island of poverty in the midst of a vast ocean of material prosperity. One hundred years later, the Negro is still languished in the corners of American society and finds himself an exile in his own land. And so we've come here today to dramatize a shameful condition.

4. In a sense we have come to our nation's capital to cash a check. When the architects of our republic wrote the magnificent words of the Constitution and the Declaration of Independence, they were signing a promissory note to which every American was to fall heir. This note was a promise that all men, yes, black men as well as white men, would be guaranteed the unalienable rights of life, liberty, and the pursuit of happiness. It is obvious today that America has defaulted on this promissory note, insofar as her citizens of color are concerned. Instead of honoring

this sacred obligation, America has given the Negro people a bad check, a check which has come back marked "insufficient funds."

5. But we refuse to believe that the bank of justice is bankrupt. We refuse to believe that there are insufficient funds in the great vaults of opportunity of this nation. And so we have come to cash this check, a check that will give us upon demand the riches of freedom and the security of justice.

6. We have also come to this hallowed spot to remind America of the fierce urgency of Now. This is no time to engage in the luxury of cooling off or to take the tranquilizing drug of gradualism. Now is the time to make real the promises of democracy. Now is the time to rise from the dark and desolate valley of segregation to the sunlit path of racial justice. Now is the time to lift our nation from the quicksands of racial injustice to the solid rock of brotherhood. Now is the time to make justice a reality for all of God's children.

7. It would be fatal for the nation to overlook the urgency of the moment. This sweltering summer of the Negro's legitimate discontent will not pass until there is an invigorating autumn of freedom and equality. Nineteen sixty-three is not an end but a beginning. Those who hope that the Negro needed to blow off steam and will now be content will have a rude awakening if the nation returns to business as usual. There will be neither rest nor tranquility in America until the Negro is granted his citizenship rights. The whirlwinds of revolt will continue to shake the foundations of our nation until the bright day of justice emerges.

8. But there is something that I must say to my people who stand on the warm threshold which leads into the palace of justice. In the process of gaining our rightful place we must not be guilty of wrongful deeds. Let us not seek to satisfy our thirst for freedom by drinking from the cup of bitterness and hatred. We must ever conduct our struggle on the high plane of dignity and discipline. We must not allow our creative protest to degenerate into physical violence. Again and again we must rise to the majestic heights of meeting physical force with soul force.

March on Washington in 1963

9. The marvelous new militancy which has engulfed the Negro community must not lead us to a distrust of all white people, for many of our white brothers, as evidenced by their presence here today, have come to realize that their destiny is tied up with our destiny. And they have come to realize that their freedom is inextricably bound to our freedom. We cannot walk alone.

10. And as we walk, we must make the pledge that we shall always march ahead. We cannot turn back. There are those who are asking the devotees of civil rights, "When will you be satisfied?" We can never be satisfied as long as the Negro is the victim of the unspeakable horrors of police brutality. We can never be satisfied as long as our bodies, heavy with the fatigue of travel, cannot gain lodging in the motels of the highways and the hotels of the cities. We cannot be satisfied as long as a Negro in Mississippi cannot vote and a Negro in New York believes he has nothing for which to vote. No, no, we are not satisfied and we will not be satisfied until justice rolls down like waters and righteousness like a mighty stream.

11. I am not unmindful that some of you have come here out of great trials and tribulations. Some of you have come fresh from narrow jail cells. Some of you have come from areas where your quest for freedom left you battered by the storms of persecutions and staggered by the winds of police brutality. You have been the veterans of creative suffering. Continue to work with the faith that unearned suffering is redemptive. Go back to Mississippi, go back to Alabama, go back to South Carolina, go back to Georgia, go back to Louisiana, go back to the slums and ghettos of our northern cities, knowing that somehow this

situation can and will be changed. Let us not wallow in the valley of despair, I say to you today, my friends. And so even though we face the difficulties of today and tomorrow, I still have a dream. It is a dream deeply rooted in the American dream.

12. I have a dream that one day this nation will rise up and live out the true meaning of its creed: We hold these truths to be self-evident that all men are created equal.

13. I have a dream that one day on the red hills of Georgia the sons of former slaves and the sons of former slave owners will be able to sit down together at the table of brotherhood.

14. I have a dream that one day even the state of Mississippi, a state sweltering with the heat of injustice, sweltering with the heat of oppression, will be transformed into an oasis of freedom and justice.

15. I have a dream that my four little children will one day live in a nation where they will not be judged by the color of their skin but by the content of their character. I have a *dream* today!

16. I have a dream that one day, down in Alabama, with its vicious racists, with its governor having his lips dripping with the words of interposition and nullification; one day right down in Alabama little black boys and black girls will be able to join hands with little white boys and white girls as sisters and brothers. I have a dream today!

17. I have a dream that one day every valley shall be exalted, and every hill and mountain shall be made low, the rough places will be made plain, and the crooked places will be made straight, and the glory of the Lord shall be revealed and all flesh shall see it together.

18. This is our hope. This is the faith that I will go back to the South with. With this faith we will be able to hew out of the mountain of despair a stone of hope. With this faith we will be able to transform the jangling discords of our nation into a beautiful symphony of brotherhood. With this faith we will be

able to work together, to pray together, to struggle together, to go to jail together, to stand up for freedom together, knowing that we will be free one day. And this will be the day, this will be the day when all of God's children will be able to sing with new meaning, "My country 'tis of thee, sweet land of liberty, of thee I sing. Land where my fathers died, land of the Pilgrim's pride, from every mountainside, let freedom ring!" And if America is to be a great nation, this must become true.

19. And so let freedom ring — from the prodigious hilltops of New Hampshire.

20. Let freedom ring — from the mighty mountains of New York.

21. Let freedom ring — from the heightening Alleghenies of Pennsylvania.

22. Let freedom ring — from the snow-capped Rockies of Colorado.

23. Let freedom ring — from the curvaceous slopes of California.

24. But not only that.

25. Let freedom ring — from Stone Mountain of Georgia. Let freedom ring — from Lookout Mountain of Tennessee.

26. Let freedom ring — from every hill and molehill of Mississippi, from every mountainside, let freedom ring!

27. And when this happens, when we allow freedom to ring, when we let it ring from every village and every hamlet, from every state and every city, we will be able to speed up that day when *all* of God's children, black men and white men, Jews and Gentiles, Protestants and Catholics, will be able to join hands and sing in the words of the old Negro spiritual,

28. "Free at last, free at last.

29. Thank *God* Almighty, we are free at last."

5. Douglas MacArthur : Farewell Speech to Congress

"Old soldiers never die they just fade away"

Apr. 19, 1951

1. I stand on this rostrum with a sense of deep humility and great pride — humility in the wake of those great architects of our history who have stood here before me, pride in the reflection that this home of legislative debate represents human liberty in the purest form yet devised.

2. Here are centered the hopes and aspirations and faith of the entire human race.

3. I do not stand here as advocate for any partisan cause, for the issues are fundamental and reach quite beyond the realm of partisan considerations. They must be resolved on the highest plane of national interest if our course is to prove sound and our future protected.

4. I trust, therefore, that you will do me the justice of receiving that which I have to say as solely expressing the considered viewpoint of a fellow American.

5. I address you with neither rancor nor bitterness in the fading twilight of life, with but one purpose in mind: to serve my country.

6. The issues are global, and so interlocked that to consider the problems of one sector oblivious to those of another is to court disaster for the whole. While Asia is commonly referred to as the gateway to Europe, it is no less true that Europe is the gateway to Asia, and the broad influence of the one cannot fail to have its impact upon the other.

7. There are those who claim our strength is inadequate to pro-

tect on both fronts, that we cannot divide our effort. I can think of no greater expression of defeatism.

8. If a potential enemy can divide his strength on two fronts, it is for us to counter his efforts. The Communist threat is a global one. Its successful advance in one sector threatens the destruction of every other sector. You cannot appease or otherwise surrender to communism in Asia without simultaneously undermining our efforts to halt its advance in Europe.

9. Beyond pointing out these general truisms, I shall confine my discussion to the general areas of Asia...

10. While I was not consulted prior to the President's decision to intervene in support of the Republic of Korea, that decision, from a military standpoint, proved a sound one.

11. As I say, it proved a sound one, as we hurled back the invader and decimated his forces. Our victory was complete, and our objectives within reach, when Red China intervened with numerically superior ground forces.

12. This created a new war and an entirely new situation, a situation not contemplated when our forces were committed against the North Korean invaders; a situation which called for new decisions in the diplomatic sphere to permit the realistic adjustment of military strategy. Such decisions have not been forthcoming.

13. While no man in his right mind would advocate sending our ground forces into continental China, and such was never given a thought, the new situation did urgently demand a drastic revision of strategic planning if our political aim was to defeat this new enemy as we had defeated the old.

14. Apart from the military need, as I saw it, to neutralize the sanctuary protection given the enemy north of the Yalu, I felt that military necessity in the conduct of the war made necessary—

15. (1) The intensification of our economic blockade against China.

16. (2) The imposition of a naval blockade against the China coast.

17. (3) Removal of restrictions on air reconnaissance of China's

coastal area and of Manchuria.

18. (4) Removal of restrictions on the forces of the republic of China on Formosa, with logistical support to contribute to their effective operations against the Chinese mainland.

19. For entertaining these views, all professionally designed to support our forces committed to Korea and to bring hostilities to an end with the least possible delay and at a saving of countless American and Allied lives, I have been severely criticized in lay circles, principally abroad, despite my understanding that from a military standpoint the above views have been fully shared in the past by practically every military leader concerned with the Korean campaign, including our own Joint Chiefs of Staff.

20. I called for reinforcements, but was informed that reinforcements were not available.

21. I made clear that if not permitted to destroy the enemy built-up bases north of the Yalu, if not permitted to utilize the friendly Chinese force of some six hundred thousand men on Formosa, if not permitted to blockade the China coast to prevent the Chinese Reds from getting succor from without, and if there were to be no hope of major reinforcements, the position of the command from the military standpoint forbade victory.

22. We could hold in Korea by constant maneuver and at an approximate area where our supply-line advantages were in balance with the supply-line disadvantages of the enemy, but we could hope at best for only an indecisive campaign with its terrible and constant attrition upon our forces if the enemy utilized his full military potential.

23. I have constantly called for the new political decisions essential to a solution.

24. Efforts have been made to distort my position. It has been said in effect that I was a warmonger. Nothing could be further from the truth.

25. I know war as few other men now living know it, and nothing to me is more revolting.

26. I have long advocated its complete abolition, as its very destructiveness on both friend and foe has rendered it useless as a means of settling international disputes.

27. Indeed, on the second day of September, 1945, just following the surrender of the Japanese nation on the battleship Missouri, I formally cautioned as follows: "Men since the beginning of time have sought peace. Various methods through the ages have been attempted to devise an international process to prevent or settle disputes between nations. From the very start workable methods were found in so far as individual citizens were concerned, but the mechanics of an instrumentality of larger international scope have never been successful.

28. "Military alliances, balances of power, leagues of nations, all in turn failed, leaving the only path to be by way of the crucible of war. The utter destructiveness of war now blocks out this alternative. We have had our last chance. If we will not devise some greater and more equitable system, our Armageddon will be at our door. The problem basically is theological and involves a spiritual recrudescence, an improvement of human character that will synchronize with our almost matchless advances in science, art, literature, and all material and cultural developments of the past two thousand years. It must be of the spirit if we are to save the flesh." But once war is forced upon us, there is no other alternative than to apply every available means to bring it to a swift end. War's very object is victory, not prolonged indecision.

29. In war there is no substitute for victory.

30. There are some who for varying reasons would appease Red China. They are blind to history's clear lesson, for history teaches with unmistakable emphasis that appeasement but begets new and bloodier war. It points to no single instance where this end has justified that means, where appeasement had led to more than a sham peace.

31. Like blackmail, it lays the basis for new and successively greater demands until, as in blackmail, violence becomes the

only alternative. Why, my soldiers asked of me, surrender military advantages to an enemy in the field? I could not answer.

32. Some may say to avoid spread of the conflict into an all-out war with China. Others, to avoid Soviet intervention. Neither explanation seems valid, for China is already engaging with the maximum power it can commit, and the Soviet will not necessarily mesh its actions with our moves. Like a cobra, any new enemy will more likely strike whenever it feels that the relativity in military or other potential is in its favor on a worldwide basis.

33. The tragedy of Korea is further heightened by the fact that its military action is confined to its territorial limits. It condemns that nation, which it is our purpose to save, to suffer the devastating impact of full naval and air bombardment while the enemy's sanctuaries are fully protected from such attack and devastation.

34. Of the nations of the world, Korea alone, up to now, is the sole one which has risked its all against communism. The magnificence of the courage and fortitude of the Korean people defies description. They have chosen to risk death rather than slavery. Their last words to me were: "Don't scuttle the Pacific."

35. I have just left your fighting sons in Korea. They have met all tests there, and I can report to you without reservation that they are splendid in every way.

36. It was my constant effort to preserve them and end this savage conflict honorably and with the least loss of time and a minimum sacrifice of life. Its growing bloodshed has caused me the deepest anguish and anxiety. Those gallant men will remain often in my thoughts and in my prayers always.

37. I am closing my fifty-two years of military service. When I joined the army, even before the turn of the century, it was the fulfillment of all my boyish hopes and dreams.

38. The world has turned over many times since I took the oath on the plain at West Point, and the hopes and dreams have long since vanished, but I still remember the refrain of one of

the most popular barracks ballads of that day which proclaimed most proudly that old soldiers never die; they just fade away.

39. And like the old soldier of that ballad, I now close my military career and just fade away, an old soldier who tried to do his duty as God gave him the light to see that duty. Good-by.